Believing in Boundaries

Using biblical teaching to understand and establish healthy modern boundaries.

Stephanie Jordan

Blessings to your journey.
Stephanie Jordan

ISBN paperback: 978-1-958441-00-8

ISBN ebook: 978-1-958441-01-5

Contents

Dedication

<u>Serenity Small Group</u>

This book is dedicated to all the ladies in my Serenity group who loved on me in my sickness of codependency—especially Synthia Morgan, who dedicated her time and energy and patience and strength for all the rest of us who needed it. I absolutely would not have had the knowledge and ability to write this book without their kick start of love and support through some really dark days.

<u>All the Relationships</u>

I'd also like to dedicate this book to everyone who taught me that I needed strong boundaries in my life. And to all the good, bad, and difficult relationships that eventually led to setting stronger boundaries in my life.

<u>My Mom</u>

She is always a supporter of my wild and crazy dreams.

My Brother

No one sees you as genuinely raw and honest as a sibling! Without him, I don't know that this project of love would have fully manifested. I appreciate the time and energy he put into helping me refine it. He is a cheerleader that inspires me to always learn and grow!

Disclaimer

I have a hyper awareness of abusive and extremely unhealthy and damaging relationships. Often people don't address these situations when they are talking about relationship issues. So before we journey into boundaries and how, I believe, God wants us to apply them, I want to address highly abusive relationships.

While this book is applicable to any relationship, based on the danger of the relationship, be it sexual, physical, or extreme verbal abuse, you may need to get help to implement these techniques into your life. Please look into local support groups. Al-anon is a great place to start, and they should have one close to or in your area. The website is listed below.

Extremely dangerous and abusive relationships do not qualify for regular relational advice or relationship practices. There is a level of safety that cannot possibly be addressed in general terms or practices. But you can access the help available. Please get help before you implement any boundaries in the relationship.

If you are in a relationship with a narcissist, boundaries will be the only thing that can bring any sort of sanity to the relationship. Please be sure to get support for narcissistic abuse recovery. Some narcissists can become dangerous when they feel like they are losing control over a situation. Please be aware and get a game plan in place before you begin to shift the relationship to make it safer and healthier for you.

You are not obligated to "work out" a relationship that is dangerous or soul sucking. I highly recommend you make a quiet game plan, with trusted people, to get away from this kind of relationship. Then if you have to have contact with this person again, your boundaries will protect you.

If you are in an abusive relationship or dangerous situation, please get help!!

The National Domestic Violence Hotline is 1-800-799-SAFE(7233).

This book is not a "how to" book on boundaries. Boundaries are as varied as the people and circumstances that you are dealing with, and I would have a difficult time covering the vastness of boundaries. I want you to understand that boundaries are important and biblical and that God is the establisher of boundaries. Understanding boundaries applied to relationships, modern cultural issues, and church culture/faith practices are my goal in sharing this book with you. I highly recommend that you find a support group to help you with your own personal journey in setting boundaries to fit your needs. Please feel free to join our online community helping to support each other. You can find the information on my website: www.believingingboundaries.com

Al-Anon's website is: https://al-anon.org

Introduction

Boundaries have been the quest of my entire adult life. I believe God called me to write this book to share my journey and encourage you, too. I struggled to navigate rocky waters without sinking because I didn't know where the rocks were and my vision was cloudy. I have spent most of my adult life shipwrecked on ridiculous rocks that could have been avoided had I just noticed the rocks to start with. It also would have helped if I had listened to the prompting in my heart that God gave me. However, I decided not to listen to the ultimate Captain of my Heartship. I actually tied up the Captain, with mutiny in my heart, and took over completely and tried to navigate all on my own. When he was talking, I duct taped his mouth and proceeded without much caution. Obviously, God is the Captain I am referring to and the ship is an analogy for my life and, ultimately, my heart.

My ship's first major rock was a broken marriage. We got married in November 1999, even though God told me not to marry him. God could see the disaster that lay ahead. But I duct taped his mouth because clearly I had this! I didn't. There was no amount of my love that was going to heal or help the brokenness in that marriage. I became a domestic violence abuse survivor. He remained a raging alcoholic. Luckily, God graciously gave me a lighthouse in the form of my firstborn son to lead me back to His direction. My son was a light in a very dark place. Two broken people do not make a whole person in a marriage. It would take me another 15 years before I learned that lesson. We divorced in August of 2003, after being separated for nearly two years.

While that was a major rock, I had many little rocks that caused dents in my heart along the way. Friendships that were unhealthy that I just couldn't walk away from. Work situations that I was too young to realize weren't OK. I was in my early 20s and truly had never heard of boundaries and didn't know that it was even a thing I should be concerned about. I was taught right and wrong, but not how sometimes wrong things (lying, deceitfulness, indifference) cross into what seem like right things (friendships, work relationships, intimate relationships). These are the rocky waters.

I was called into my second marriage to my late husband, Jay. We married in June of 2004. We were both fervently living for God, and the Captain was definitely manning the Heartship. I think we got married in calm waters, but we immediately tied up and duct taped the Captain and traveled directly into some major storms. I say I think it was calm waters, because looking back on that time in my life, I am not sure much was calm. It was a beautiful collision of two beat-up ships handcrafted into one ship. God took the broken pieces of each of our ships and put them together to make us stay afloat. Remember that I said two broken people don't make a whole person? It applies here too. Our Craftsman was repairing us individually, but He had to start with the broken parts that were there to work with. So off we went with a tied up and duct taped Captain into a night that would last years. Within a month of our marriage, I was pregnant with our baby girl. I had a lot of trauma from my first marriage, especially with pregnancy because of physical abuse while pregnant, and I was completely freaked out and terrified to be in that situation again. Pregnant by a man, vulnerable to a man. I still knew absolutely nothing about boundaries and how they applied to life. We became involved in a church at that time that had a recovery ministry. I started attending the Serenity groups every Wednesday night. Serenity is a Christian small group at the church I attended at the time that is based on the Twelve-step program used for recovery from addiction and codependency. This group became a lifeline for me, and for the first time ever, I realized my part of the addiction cycle of sickness, and it included a serious lack of boundaries.

In 2006, Jay relapsed on drugs. He used drugs for that entire year until he went to rehab in November. The Serenity group helped me set my boundaries. I didn't have to accept his terms or his use because it was dangerous and unhealthy for our entire family. This boundary seems obvious, right? But nothing is clear when you are living in the chaos. The chaos clouds the line of healthy and unhealthy boundaries in relationships. I absolutely hated his guts, and I was angry at God for calling me into a ridiculous marriage. I felt like God had thrown me into the rocks this time. Why?! Why did he throw me into the rocks when I had fought so long and hard to get off the previous rocks on which I had been shipwrecked? How could he do this to me?

I got pregnant with my third baby, a boy, while Jay was in rehab. My son was prophesied, so I knew he was coming. I was still surprised by the timing, though I have come to learn that God's timing looks absolutely nothing like perfect timing. Home Jay came. I don't know that either of us really knew what to do with this situation. I was exhausted. I had set some hard boundaries that were definitely beneficial for us, and it helped Jay from ever revisiting his habit. Jay and I had two more children, for a total of four kids together. He raised my firstborn like he was his own. I think God kept giving us children because He knew we needed more than a sheet of paper (i.e., a marriage license) to keep this crazy train together. We both still had so much brokenness that we continued for many years, nearly a decade, with some painful situations. But going through those situations is what God used to give me a passion for boundaries, grace, and forgiveness and what, eventually, led to this book. In December 2014, Jay passed away suddenly from hypertension, an event that was especially traumatic for me.

After all that, I still have to fight my codependent tendencies in relationships. But, oh, how far I have come! I am much better at setting boundaries for my needs and not allowing others to be selfish. I have had to have some strong conversations with people who think my boundaries are "harsh" and question why can't I give a little. The reason is "giving a little" only has a place in a healthy relationship, not an unhealthy one. In a healthy relationship, there is give on both sides and a recognition of needs on both sides. But in an unhealthy one if you choose to give a little, you have to be willing to absorb all the consequences that come with the give. I am no longer willing to absorb those consequences to the demise of my own heart and needs. My journey will never end because my prone is to "give a little" a bit too often and a bit too much.

Part one:

Understanding boundaries

Chapter 1

Becoming a Believer

The boundary principles that you will learn throughout this book are valid and useful for anyone and everyone, believer in Christ and non-believer. However, with the power of the Holy Spirit inside to help teach, lead, guide, and open your eyes to needs, your path will be more illuminated and you will have the strength needed to carry out your plan and create healthy boundaries for yourself. God allowed Jesus to come to Earth to create the ability for the Holy Spirit to live inside of us. Prior to Christ's death and resurrection, humans didn't have the same direct connection to God. We had to either make sacrifices ourselves or visit a place called The Holy of Holies (Exodus 26:33), both of which constituted major boundaries between God and mankind. The Holy of Holies was inside the temple, where the presence of God dwelt with His people until Christ came along. The Holy of Holies had a veil around it. See, it was such a dense presence of God that you would die if you entered without first being consecrated unto God (Exodus 33:20), and only the high priest dared to enter in. He wore a rope tied around his waist so if God found him to be unclean and killed him, the "commoners" could extract him

3

without subjecting themselves to the power found in the inner sanctum. When Christ died on the cross, the veil in the temple ripped from top to bottom (Matthew 27:51). This wasn't like a tiny curtain that was see-through. This veil was at least three feet thick and made by excellent craftsmen with the finest of fabrics. The power of the redemption of the cross ripped that veil wide open for you, me, and all those who call on the name of Jesus so we may enter into The Holy of Holies with our Father (Luke 23:45). God is a big fan of boundaries. He knows that we are safe with boundaries. When he removed the boundary of the veil between us, He replaced it with the powerful cleansing blood of Jesus Christ (a sacrificial boundary) that offers us the ultimate freedom through forgiveness of our sins.

Christ did the work that we can never do for ourselves. He took all the ugly that we will ever do and cleaned it away through his sacrifice so we could have life to the fullest (John 10:10). Christ didn't come just to redeem us. He came to get the keys to Death and Hades (Revelation 1:18) so those spiritual principles no longer had power or control over us, his brothers and sisters.

The work of Christ having victory over Death and Hades is such an important thing because as we set boundaries with our loved ones, sometimes we will have to accept that they may die in their behavior. This acceptance is one of *the hardest* to face on the boundary journey, yet so critical for freedom for your heart and for the person whom you are "trying to save." You, my sweet friend, do not have the power to save anyone. God does. Sometimes, he needs you to get out of his way so he can do that very thing. It is still up to the person whether to choose to get help and be saved or not. I had to learn to accept this with my late husband, Jay, who had a longtime love affair with drugs prior to meeting me. I had to be

OK if he died of his addiction during his relapse in the beginning of our marriage. I had to allow him to make the decision whether he wanted to get help and live or whether he was going to die in his addiction. As I got healthier and quit trying to control him, rescue him, and make everything OK, he had to face himself. During that time, I had to set firm boundaries with him. He was no longer able to see our children, come to our house, or have anything to do with us outside of visitation at a public place. It was when he realized I wasn't going to bend that he began to realize his need for help. Praise the Lord that he chose to go to rehab. He chose. He made the effort. He finally was able to conquer his addiction tendencies that he struggled with his whole life. Thankfully, he lived through it. Though he still had struggles, the Holy Spirit gave him the strength to stay strong.

Jesus' final loving act was to leave here so our helper, the Holy Spirit, could come (John 16:7). We are spiritual beings. We have a space built inside of us that is meant to be filled with a spirit. You may have heard it referred to as the "God-shaped hole." It is absolutely designed to be filled with God, but we try to fill it with all sorts of other odd-shaped things: love, sex, money, drugs, power, material belongings, our children. When we try to satisfy ourselves with things that do not have the power or ability to fill that specifically shaped hole, we will be left wanting. They are too shallow, too small, too big or out of shape for the hole. God designed us this way because when He made us, we were made to be in perfect unison with Him. Our Creator. Our Father.

When we accept Jesus' redemption in our lives and walk through the torn veil, I mean in a spiritual sense, not an actual physical act, we immediately get our God-shaped hole filled with the Holy Spirit, the power player of the Trinity. The Trinity is God the

Father, Jesus the Son, and the Holy Spirit. When the Holy Spirit comes and abides in us, we have the power to do so much that we can't do on our own. One thing we have the power to do with the aid of the Spirit is set healthy boundaries. We are able to rest in the love of God and understand that God has boundaries and that he will do work on our behalf, but we just have to trust him. We must lay ourselves down and release ourselves from trying to be God to someone else. We cannot fill their God-shaped hole either. We damage ourselves and them when we try.

If you haven't accepted Jesus Christ, please say this prayer with me and begin today a new walk with God and to be filled with the Holy Spirit.

Lord God,
Thank you for allowing your Son, Jesus, to come and be my
propitiation to You. I believe that Jesus has completed my salvation
through his sacrifice on the cross. I believe you rose from death as
conqueror of Death and Hades. I have sinned, and now I fully turn
away from my former behaviors and will follow you with my life. I
accept Jesus as my Lord and Savior of my life.
In Jesus' name,
Amen

Chapter 2

God Shows Us How Important Boundaries Are

I gave the example for the veil being a boundary that God had set up, but God set up even more boundaries. Let's start with creation:

> *"In the beginning, God created the heavens and the earth. The earth was formless and void and darkness was over the surface of the deep and the Spirit of God was moving over the surface of the waters. Then God said, 'Let there be light' and there was light. God saw that the light was good and God separated the light from the darkness. God called the light day and the darkness he called night. There was evening and there was morning, one day" (Genesis 1:1–5 NASB).*

When the earth was first created, it was formless, void, and dark. Then God created the light. When He saw that the light was good, He *separated* it from darkness. He set the boundaries of light and dark. In his wisdom, He knows that we depend on light and dark. If you live far enough north or south on this planet, you will have up to six months of light and long periods of time of darkness. I can't imagine having to acclimate to that, but I find it so interesting that the people who live there have to compensate for their awkward changing of seasons. I'm sure many of them sleep with something over their eyes or a pillow over their head or perhaps blackout curtains in the summer, and in the winter, they must depend on artificial light to make their days happen. Darkness is a fundamental part of our schedules, and light is often the reminder that it is time to function and be productive.

> *"Then God said, 'Let there be an expanse in the midst of the waters and let it separate the waters from the waters.' God made the expanse and separated the waters which were below the expanse from the waters which were above the expanse and it was so. God called the expanse heaven. There was evening and there was morning, the second day" (Genesis 1:6–8 NASB).*

This is where God created the skies and clouds and upper atmosphere and the ocean waters and other bodies of water below. The clouds still feed the oceans with their rain. The ocean waters evaporate to form the clouds. The clouds move the ocean in so many ways; the oceans move the clouds in so many ways. It is fascinating how God separated them but didn't disconnect them.

They are still interactive and important to each other. However, they have their boundaries set in place. In a similar way, we can have boundaries without disconnection.

> *"Then God said, 'Let the waters below the heavens be gathered into one place and let the dry land appear,' and it was so. God called the dry land earth and the gathering of the waters he called the seas. God saw that it was good. Then God said, 'Let the earth sprout vegetation: plants yielding seeds and fruit trees on the earth bearing fruit after their own kind with seed in them,' and it was so. The earth brought forth vegetation . . ." (Genesis 1:9–13 NASB).*

God set the boundaries of the seas and the earth. When the ocean violates these boundaries, it will create chaos. Tsunamis and tidal waves show us how important it is to maintain the boundaries of the earth and seas. When a tsunami hits land and crosses the boundary of dry land, it leaves nothing but utter destruction in its wake. It is the same principle when we allow someone to violate our boundaries. We will often be left with a wake of destruction, and we feel violated, angry, and insecure.

"Then God said, 'Let there be lights in the expanse of the heavens to separate the day from the night, and let them be for signs and for the seasons and for days and years; and let them be for lights in the expanse of the heavens to give light on the earth' and it was so. God made the two great lights, the greater light to govern the day and the lesser light to govern the night. He made the stars also ..." (Genesis 1:14–19 NASB).

Anybody else find it totally fascinating how the moon picks up the sun's light without being overbearing? In his mastery, God set the sun, this massive light that is so powerful and strong, just far enough away that it doesn't burn us up but gives life. It provides light and life to the Earth, but then, in such graciousness, comes the cool of the night with just enough light, as the moon borrows the sun's glare, to make us ready to sleep.

I live in the southern part of the United States. It can get so very hot here. Some days are easily 100 degrees Fahrenheit in the summer with enough humidity in the air that it feels like you are breathing water. There is nothing better on those days than the coolness that the night can bring. It is a beautiful dance between the heat of day and the release of the sun to let the moon settle in and cool the world down since it provides no direct light on its own. We depend on this rotation so much that if for some reason the sun didn't rise in the morning or the night didn't come, we would be fearful of what would happen if the devastation wasn't immediate. Boundaries, in all ways, keep us safe.

Chapter 3

Where Do We Need Boundaries?

The boundaries mentioned in the last chapter were physical. These boundaries are so much easier to see because they are tangible, but these other boundaries can't necessarily be seen. We need boundaries in areas that affect us closely, and in our daily lives.

Relationship boundaries are also a bit more complex and abstract than physical boundaries. Relationship boundaries can be some of the hardest boundaries to create because you may be intimately involved with the person on some level. Relational boundaries that we recognize include the generations, such as grandparents, parents, and children; less direct relations, such as cousins; and indirect relations, such as in-laws. We don't expect young children to be taking care of their parents, and we hope that grandparents can be fun and not have to do the raising of their grandchildren. Friends are another example of relational boundaries. We know that if someone is not blood related, they are not technically family, even if they can seem like family and sometimes even feel more like family. Genetic family is not a relationship that we can choose. It is given to us. Friends, however, we are able to choose. You may be one of the people that were given friendships that maybe seem like you didn't choose them, nor did you have the option, but I promise, if you set some boundaries, it might help clean those relationships up and weed out the ones you don't need.

Throughout the book, I will touch on boundaries with parents, spouses, children, and friends, as well as more distant relationships, like coworkers, bosses, and employees.

Unfortunately, people rarely naturally honor others' boundaries or even recognize that the boundaries are there at all. Why? Why is it that we don't see or acknowledge boundaries? Well, unless we are taught boundaries, we don't even recognize them for ourselves, so how can we possibly recognize them for others? There is a dance, if you will, in every relationship, but sometimes when we haven't been taught how to dance, we step on toes, a boundary violation. While we must take the time to learn about others' boundaries, we must first establish our own. Once you begin to see how beneficial boundaries are, you then are not offended by someone else's boundaries. You can respect their need to protect themselves, their thoughts, their family and whatever boundary is in place to keep them safe.

Cultural boundaries are important because our culture shapes us as people. We can either allow culture to have full influence, maybe without even recognizing how much influence it has in shaping us, or we can recognize areas where cultural influences cross lines and we hold our place safely with boundaries. In this social media world, it is critical to maintain healthy boundaries and not allow others to push over them. Whether you realize it right now or not, you *have* boundaries established. You know when you get upset because someone said or did something to harm you or upset you. You know it enrages you, and you immediately go on the defense. This indicates a boundary has been crossed. Perhaps you just didn't have that line drawn dark enough to know that is why you were so upset. Our cultural experience currently is so flipped upside down that often we don't even know what to do or say. We feel attacked from every direction. It's OK; you will soon know how to stand your ground and the importance of it so you can navigate those rocky waters way more clearly.

Faith practice boundaries also are important to keep us grounded as we develop relationships and even operate our faith practices. I know it may seem silly, but church hurt is a really big issue today. The term "church hurt" comes from issues that have caused heartache, heartbreak, or division in the church. I know that we would love to all just get along and see things eye to eye and have kumbaya moments, but that just isn't the reality of human relationships. So what are safe boundaries with your pastor, fellow church members, and leaders? Just like with cultural boundaries, we often have established these but haven't recognized that the hurt comes from not having them drawn dark enough. Our fellow brothers and sisters will step on our toes, and we have no idea how to handle it. We will look the other way, turn the cheek, yet we feel completely violated. Our pastors will speak something that makes us feel uncomfortable or they are overly controlling, and we can't put our finger on it exactly, but in our heart of hearts, we know that it seems off. How do you tell the guy who is in control of the church "flock" that he's wrong? What about the little lady that always makes a comment on how you look? How your kids look? Is she insulting you or is she just pointing things out? You don't know. You can't tell what her intentions are, so you feel confused and perhaps insulted, but she's the nice little old lady at church (that you dread coming your way). These are the instances in which recognizing your boundaries and being able to hold them strongly is critical.

These boundaries help us protect our faith from becoming subjective to others' interpretations or opinions about what scripture says. We must have a Godly perspective when we read the Word. Universalism is one area that boundaries in our faith practices are critical. The open concept can lead our hearts astray from truth that is found in the Bible.

Church and politics can become dangerous grounds for losing our testimony and shining the glory of God. When we set boundaries around our political beliefs to make sure they align with our faith, we will keep balance

Boundaries are important in relationships, culture, and faith, and in other areas of our life. God set and held boundaries so it is Biblical and OK to hold your line. God sets a hard line and doesn't apologize for it because he knows it is for our good, and it keeps us being able to trust him. How could we trust God if he wavers regularly? How would we know where to stand if today it's OK, but tomorrow it isn't? What if we are crossing lines, but He never tells us that we are? We can never feel safe in a relationship that has no boundaries, which is why a relationship with God is always safe.

Chapter 4

What Are Boundaries?

Now that we have discussed where boundaries are necessary, answering the what question is critical. What are boundaries?

Dictionary.com states that a boundary is something that indicates bounds or limits. The definition for bounds is a limit, something that restrains or confines. The use of the word "limit" is probably the reason most people don't practice boundaries or don't want to acknowledge them. In our culture today, there is a corrupted thought of free everything. We have free speech; we have free purchases, as in "buy one, get one free"; and we are constantly talking about "free" money and who should receive it. We are on the far side of the free love movement of the 1960s, but it seems that love became free or was given out too easily then, and we have never learned to rein it back in. Why would we want something that restrains, confines, or limits us?

Good question. We have boundaries in our lives all the time. We appreciate those boundaries and understand the need for them. For example, our world has boundaries. We have land masses and ocean waters. We recognize that we can't just build cities on top of the water masses because 1) we would be completely destroying the habitat and 2) the water is more volatile than land. We settle ourselves within the boundaries of land because it is the safest and most logical place for us to build and grow our cultures.

Then within each of those land masses, we have additional boundaries: continents, countries, states, provinces, counties, parishes, and cities. Of course, the smallest boundary that we have for space is our very own home. Within your home, there are floors, walls, and ceilings that provide additional physical boundaries for safety, privacy, and protection. Your home may be large and vast, or it may be small and compact, but no matter, it is your home and you feel safe in it. You definitely do not want the boundaries of your home to be violated at any time. Likewise, we do not cross our neighbor's front door without an invitation into their home.

When boundaries of countries are violated, countries often go to war. Why? Because maintaining that boundary is critical. When boundaries of a city are violated, the police are probably involved. When the boundaries of our home are violated, we look for ways to protect ourselves and others in our home. To violate a clear boundary line is often called an offense. After all, we feel offended when others have crossed our boundaries, although we didn't know that we had a line there.

What are relationship boundaries?

We can see the need to restrain or confine when it comes to outward territories, but what about the territory of our heart? Proverbs 4:23 tells us to guard our hearts with diligence because the springs of life flow from it. It is so important, critical really, that we guard our hearts, that we put boundaries around our hearts. From our heart flows the springs of life and that is a poetic metaphor for our speech, our relationships, our behaviors. These help us to navigate our life.

If you look at much of our world today, you can see that relational boundaries are, by far, the hardest to maintain properly and that we tend to get really messy in the relational department. So many families today have no lines at all to create healthy individuals. We have fathers who are absent and so children aren't guided by their head of household. We have moms working their tails off and not able to invest in the life lessons kids need. We have grandparents raising their grandkids because the parents are too self-absorbed to do it. It is a mess!

We understand boundaries in the physical context and we understand the need to protect boundary lines. So why can't we do that with our relationships? Why does it feel like we are wrong to create definitive lines in relationships? It's because relationships are fluid. They feel much more like building a city on water than they do building it on solid ground. For instance, our relationships change over the years, even with the people we have known the longest. Some relationships get closer, but many disappear altogether. Heaven forbid that we are rejected, especially by our own merits, though it may not be our fault!

When our hearts aren't guided by the safe boundaries that we need to definitively set into place, we tend to become a mess in the "springs of life" department. We have brokenness everywhere, and we allow offense to grow because we are unprotected. We may live in rocky waters, but we don't have to get taken down by them. We can create healthy boundaries for ourselves. You can create healthy boundaries for yourself. It is OK. It is necessary. It is healthy.

<u>Just say no</u>

The most common, well-respected, and pronounced boundary is the word *no*. No is a perfectly acceptable boundary, and the beginning of all boundaries. Many people fear telling others no, but hopefully, by the end of this book, you will feel much more comfortable with saying no to situations, thought processes, relationships, cultural issues, and faith practices that make you feel uncomfortable.

No is a simple word, but it is very powerful. When you say no to someone or something, it does not mean that you are rejecting the person, personally. It is not an attack against the person but a line stating what works best for you.

No, I will not get involved in that situation.
No, I will not allow you to speak to me that way.
No, I will not take you anywhere.
No, I will not work on that project on my off time.
No, I cannot travel this weekend.
No, I will not be a classroom mom.

Whatever you may need to say no to in order to keep your boundaries safe and healthy for yourself is important. Do not let the fear of others keep you from using this potent two-letter word, no. When you start establishing this boundary with others that are not used to it, they may be shocked or angry with you, but that does not change your answer. You can't let them push your boundary back because they are uncomfortable with your established boundary. Give yourself grace and time to learn to be comfortable with saying no to others. Just start with one no. But hold to it. Do not give in, no matter what! You can do it! Whew! Doesn't that feel good? I know you can make a better, safer future for you and your family by practicing setting boundaries and telling others no when you need to.

Chapter 5

Why Do We Need Boundaries?

Having covered the where and the what, I will touch on the why. We will dig into this answer as the book unfolds, but I think touching on it now is good. When we are looking at the boundaries, say for a country, we see the need to have that line. It shows us where things change and where safety is. For example, if you are in a war zone and you need to get out of it, the only way to know how to do that is to know where the line is. When our relationships look like war zones, you have to have a line in place to know how to get out of it.

Your boundaries are set for you, not for others. They keep you safe. The focus is not for others. You cannot control others and what they need. You only have control over you and your behaviors. Talk about a rude awakening! When I realized that I couldn't control others and I had to learn to only control myself and my responses, I had to sit and reflect on it a bit. Controlling others doesn't work. We find false logic in our attempts: If I pitch a fit loudly enough, they will do what I want. If I just call them on the phone one million times, they will surely do what I want. If I just don't talk to them at all, they will do what I want. None of this works. It usually just leaves us irritated and aggressive with no real resolution to the issue. This is called codependency, which according to Dictionary.com relates to a relationship in which one or more person is physically or psychologically addicted, as to alcohol or gambling, and the other person is psychologically dependent on the first in an unhealthy way This is where the rubber meets the road with the need for boundaries. When I didn't have defined lines, no one else knew what my lines were either.

Without boundaries, we find ourselves in codependent relationships. We become addicted to the need to control or enable someone by making excuses for or defending their poor behavior. We often regulate our own feelings and emotions by how the other person is doing. If he/she is OK, then we can be OK too. If he/she isn't OK, then our world is spiraling out of control as well. The sickness of codependency is what propels the need for boundaries. Codependency is the crux of why to establish boundaries.

What is a codependent relationship

There are typically three different types of codependents: controlling, enabling, and then the hybrid controlling-enabling. Controlling codependents tend to think as long as they have control of a situation, they will be able to control the person. A controlling codependent may pay for everything, or dominate time, or be demanding, or all three simultaneously. Often this person will look like they are in control and have their stuff together, but usually their mental health is dependent on how well the other person's life is going. I fall into this category, because I always seemed to have my stuff together, while I was just helping them (my ex and my late husband) out. I just wanted them to be ok. Really what I wanted was to make sure that they were ok, so I could be ok. I was never ok. They were never ok. We were sick together. There was no amount of bailing out of jail that was going to get my ex-husband to see that he had a drinking problem. There was no amount of begging to get help that was going to change anything. There was no amount of phone calls that was going to stop my late husband from doing whatever he wanted to do. I just felt like I needed to control the situation, and then it would all be better. It never was. The more control I presumed I had, the more miserable I was because they were not upholding their end of the deal. They were not doing what they were supposed to be doing. I had set that up in my own mind. I had made the scenario in my head and we were all playing the roles except they were doing it poorly. They weren't behaving. I was angry and disappointed. Realizing I had no control was a devastating and freeing realization. I no longer had to make sure that they were doing the right thing so that I could go about my day.

Enabling codependents typically enables the other person by "fixing" everything for them. The other person will rarely or never have to face consequences for bad behaviors or misconduct. Enabling codependents will rescue others to their own demise. For example, a dad who spends every penny he has to take care of a child who won't work or provide for their family or won't stop using drugs. A friend who constantly feels the need to take a friend to work even though it interrupts what she should be doing but she feels guilty if she doesn't do it. The friend may also play on her feelings and manipulate her into feeling guilty because she isn't doing his/her bidding. Enabling codependents usually are kind and have high guilt complexes. A guilt complex is being able to be motivated or manipulated by the use of guilt. Enablers are usually mostly manipulated by the use of guilt. Many will feel like they are just loving on other people and helping them out. In theory, that is a good thing, but only in a healthy relationship. It is codependency when the other person doesn't respect your boundaries and will use your feelings against you to force you to do what they want regardless of your needs. Enabling codependents need to release the feelings of guilt and shame. You cannot take care of the whole world.

The hybrid is more commonly someone in an authority position over the other person, e.g., a parent or spouse that has more means than the other. But there are truly no limits when there is sickness in the relationship and enablers may fluctuate back and forth into the hybrid category as well as typically controlling codependents. However, the hybrid is definitely in its own category. For example, it might be a mom who gets their child an apartment, and then when the child does something that she doesn't like, she takes the apartment away. When the dust settles from that fight, she gets her another apartment. Then takes it away. Sets the child up again, and then takes it out from underneath the child. Setting the child up is the enabling part. The mom resents that the child isn't able to stand alone but also feels a sense of guilt that she should be taking care of the child's needs. The act of removing the stability as needed is the control part. The mom likes knowing she can have her say in whatever the child does and always threatens the lack of security. She feels like she can make the child behave with her threats. She follows through with the threats, not to maintain boundaries, but to prove she is in control. Holding boundaries would be once she removed the first apartment, she never did anything else to help because she realizes that the cycle of setting up and removal is unhealthy and tiring for both parties.

All three types of codependency are a sickness. Sometimes, our codependency wants us to have all the glory for all the efforts we are making to help another's life be better. This is a symptom of the sickness of codependency. If we were truly healthy in our approach, then 1) we would realize that the issue isn't really our issue to start with, and 2) we would help without needing recognition. I am sure you have heard it from people you are around. It may sound something like this, "I help them all the time," or "If they would just pull themselves together, they wouldn't need me anymore," or "I wish they didn't always call to ask me for help." These statements tend to lend themselves to a victim-mentality of helping others. There is no sense that they got the opportunity to bless someone but more that by helping them, they were taken advantage of in some way. The person who makes these statements usually has made someone else's problem their problem too many times and now resents it.

Need for boundaries in codependent relationships

Codependency is one of those conditions that "other" people have. It isn't a disease you catch, but it is certainly a disease of the mind. When we are in a codependent relationship, we think we don't have *that* issue. We say, "I just loved the person, and I just wanted to help him or her." Sound familiar? Loving someone who is sick in some way, be it toxic for you, addicted to a substance, needing more than you have to give repetitively, is a recipe for codependency.

And when we are in a codependent relationship, boundaries are critical. This may seem trivial, but when we give in to keep the peace at all costs, we are compromising our standards and our hearts. After a period of time, especially compromising our hearts, we will be miserable and wonder why our lives look nothing like they should and will constantly think, "How did I get here?" This thinking means that we haven't been in control of our lives because we let others be in control, and now we are unhappy. It is not the other person's fault that we gave them control. We freely, even if unknowingly, gave it to them. That doesn't mean that we can't take it back. We can, and must, absolutely take back the control of our lives and relinquish the pseudo-control of other people's lives.

Maybe your child just needs, needs, needs, from you, and you are exhausted but feel like it's your duty because they are your child. Well, those are good intentions that come out of a good place; however, you must ask yourself, "How old is my child? Should he or she be self-sufficient by now? Does this relationship exhaust me?" If your answers are:

1) over 25 and not self-sufficient (yes, 18 is technically an adult, but there is some leeway as they learn to stand on their own two feet) and 2) this relationship exhausts me, you might be codependent with your child. This is just one example, but you can ask yourself some variation of these questions with all the relationships in your life to find the answer. The biggest question being, "Does this relationship exhaust me?"

Read that again. And again. And again. You are now aware of one possible issue that brought you to read this book in the first place. If you are in a codependent relationship, you need boundaries. Period. Maybe you see your codependency as being nice. Maybe you see it as loving others. That was typically my issue. I mostly experienced codependency through marriage relationships, and I loved the men in my life so I wanted them to be OK. But I just made myself crazy trying to *make* them OK. I couldn't do that *for* them. I couldn't be the one to heal, fix, or help them, but dang it, I nearly made myself crazy trying to do so. Until one day, through the Serenity group, the lightbulb went off and I realized that I am not responsible for anyone else's feelings, life, or behaviors and I don't have to be fully affected by them. Wow! What a relief! But then the journey to understand what it meant to not be fully responsible for someone else and putting it into practice began. The theory of not being responsible for someone else's action, feelings, and behaviors turning into practical life practices took some time to develop. It may take time and that is OK. The world's international boundaries weren't established overnight, and sometimes they have to change a little with the changing of the times. Yours may be similar. It may take some time to recognize which relationships need some firm boundary lines, establishing the boundaries with people, and then changing them as needed as the relationship shifts.

For example, I will stick with the parent/child codependent relationship: Your 30-year-old son lives in your garage and wants his girlfriend to move in, knowing that it is against your rules. You tell him no. He presses and keeps pressing. However since you've given in so many times, he's pretty sure you will this time too. Yet you hold your boundary, which is no girlfriends living in the house. He ramps up the anger because you aren't giving in. He starts pitching fits and is now almost impossible to talk to because you won't give him his way. This is how he has learned to control. It has always worked in the past. You gave in to him to make him settle down. You gave in so that you didn't have to deal with his fits. You gave in because it was easier. Instead of giving in this time though, you draw a hard line and tell him to move out. He's shocked! He didn't expect that. Living with you has given him the freedom to do whatever he wants to do while you absorb the responsibilities of the household, so he never even considered moving out. If you see your line as bendable or moveable, then he will probably push until he finds the breaking point. If your line is solid, without any vulnerable spots, then he will learn that he can't take advantage of you anymore.

To hold your boundary line, you need to realize their emergencies or situations are no longer your responsibility. When they have issues, you no longer rescue them.

You may be thinking, "Well, that sounds cold!" We are not talking about healthy interactions in relationships. We are talking about an unhealthy relationship. I don't think anyone questions a city upholding its boundaries when it comes to protecting its citizens. It isn't cold to protect yourself from a situation/relationship that is creating craziness and instability in your life. Not to hold those boundaries and protect yourself is only living in foolishness and ignorance. Your codependency is probably an issue for others as well. It is often all consuming and it requires others to help at times when they feel like the person you want to help should no longer be helped. So if you are thinking that setting boundaries and removing yourself from an unhealthy situation is cold, then I implore you to keep reading!

In some scenarios, things can get a lot more dangerous and scary before they get better. It really depends on how deep the codependency is. This can make it harder to hold the line, although it is *critical* to do so. You may need help and a support system. Please take the time to find someone who will hold you accountable, and to help keep you safe should a dangerous situation arise.

Protection from Manipulation

We need boundaries to protect us against manipulation. People who are crossing your boundaries are manipulating something to work for themselves. It is a manipulation of your feelings, security, fears, insecurities, and relationships. Everyone manipulates, at times, to get their way, whether intentionally or unintentionally. Manipulation is a natural human sin nature. When you start setting healthy boundaries, you more easily see the areas in which you will try to manipulate others and the areas in which others will try to manipulate you. And you will begin to see unhealthy relationships change or disappear altogether. People who want to have a healthy relationship will begin to appreciate and accept your boundaries and potentially even have conversations with you about how your boundaries are affecting them so you can come to a healthy place for both parties. It will start to blow your mind how you no longer resent relationships and you no longer dread meeting new people because you are healthy enough to set the lines that make you feel safe from the start.

The good news is you can actually tell people what your boundaries are. You can share them as much as necessary to set the dark line for others to see. Let's say that you plan on meeting someone new at a coffee shop. In the past, you have had to get the bill for someone because they forgot their money. It wasn't just once, but it always seemed to happen every time the two of you hung out. You started to resent hanging out with that person. Eventually you quit because you didn't feel safe telling that friend that you weren't OK with footing the bill every time y'all hung out. Before you meet your new friend, you could have an honest conversation and tell him/her that you will only be paying your way for the day, so he/she needs to make sure to bring his/her wallet. It may seem forward, but what a relief it is when you can just enjoy the day and know that you won't be put on the spot again. Another way to handle it, if the situation arises, is at the moment you can say, "I'm sorry. I don't feel comfortable starting out our friendship by paying your way. Is there someone you can call to help you pay?"

Sometimes you don't state your boundary exactly, but you just hold your line. For example, I had a friend on Facebook try to rope me into a debate the other day. He made a post of a video on his page that shared a different viewpoint than mine and then tagged me in it and asked what I thought. I knew he was trying to rope me into a debate on a public forum. So I answered that the author of the original post and I probably have very little in common and I would probably heavily debate her. He answered back and asked me why I thought that the author and I had nothing in common. See, I never said that we had *nothing* in common to begin with. He had twisted my words. He wasn't listening. Because he was only trying to stir up the mess pot, I told him that if he would like to move to a private message, I would be happy to talk with him. He told me that he wouldn't "coddle" me by having a private conversation. So I told him that I didn't owe him a conversation on a public forum, and if he thought that having a private conversation on a highly controversial topic affecting our nation was "coddling," then we treat our relationships very differently and that is OK, but I would not be participating. He doesn't get to force me into a conversation that I know will be hurtful and unproductive. He doesn't get to set the standard by which I will or will not share myself. Only I get to set that standard and boundary. I didn't have the conversation with him publicly or privately, and I am much better in my heart for it. I could've gotten roped in. I could've poured myself out and let the wolves come and pick away at me. But at what cost? My peace. My heart. My mental health. It wasn't worth that sacrifice. So leaving him unsatisfied was fine for me, and it was up to him to determine what he should do on his end. It was wonderfully freeing to be able to establish my boundaries and hold to them. I didn't tell him that my boundary was that I get to choose what I share, but I held to my boundary nonetheless. So you can either tell people your boundaries or just hold to them.

Either way, they are not easy to hold. They are just necessary to hold. If you aren't a bold personality, it may be harder for you to start, but once you start, you will never want to go back! You will be so thankful and feel safe in your relationships and so your gentle personality can actually shine instead of feeling the need to be protective. You will have to protect yourself in some way when dealing with others, so establish and hold boundaries, or you will be miserable if you don't establish them. It is best to go ahead and set your boundaries up from the beginning of relationships or as soon as you can with established relationships.

Chapter 6

Job's Lesson on Boundaries

If you've never read the book of Job, I highly recommend it. The book is full of trials and devastation. Job lost everything. Every. Single. Thing. The worst part of it all is that it was like a setup. Job was doing everything right, so Satan just wanted to wreck him because he could. Because Job was an honest and God-loving man, Satan hated him for it. But again, God set a boundary and that was Satan could not take Job's life. Job's struggles seem cruel in ways, and I have struggled with it at times. However, we are here for God's glory, God is not here for our glory, and in the end, Job is shown God's glory in the most amazing way. Just like a Father who has had to teach his child a hard lesson, God does this with Job and then brings redemption that only God can do. Job gets everything back sevenfold. You better believe Job cherished every single bit of it better. I'm sure Job never forgot what he lost or his journey to get where he ended up and had a humility that is awe-inspiring.

So here we have poor Job in the ash heap, weeping, wailing . . . really just making a huge fuss about his losses. Who could blame him? He was a hot mess! Covered in boils and wounds, his family dead, and his life destroyed, he had to stand up against his friends who were encouraging him to curse God and die. His friends were like, "Yo Job! This isn't getting any better and clearly God hates you, so why don't you go ahead and curse God so you can just die and get this craziness over with!!" But Job *knew* at his core that God is good and faithful and that something was up, something greater than himself. He wasn't about to curse God, but he did expect God to start answering him. He started questioning God and was crying out pleading for an answer to his plight.

Job's boundaries had been violated in all sorts of ways by the tragedies, but these were not things in his control. We can't control anyone else's life or death. We can't control whether we are prosperous in our work. We can't control everything, and what Job lost he didn't have control over. So Job was grappling for what he thought he could control. He wanted answers. Why me?! What did I do to you?! Why would you do this to someone who has been faithful to you?! Why didn't you save them?! Why didn't you prevent this from happening?! Do these questions sound familiar? Thinking you have control where only God has control will leave you asking these very questions over and over again.

Then God answers. The very first thing God tells Job is to "gird up your loins" or "tighten your belt." So in that era, that was like telling him to get ready for battle. It was a charge to him. Basically, get up and put on your big boy undies 'cause we are about to throw down in Job 38: 1–41:

> [1]Then the Lord answered Job from the whirlwind and said,
> [2]"Who is this who darkens the divine plan
> By words without knowledge?
> [3]Now tighten the belt on your waist like a man,
> And I shall ask you, and you inform Me!

[4]Where were you when I laid the foundation of the earth?
Tell Me, if you have understanding,

[5]Who set its measurements? Since you know.
Or who stretched the measuring line over it?
[6]On what were its bases sunk?
Or who laid its cornerstone,
[7]When the morning stars sang together
And all the sons of God shouted for joy?

[8]"Or who enclosed the sea with doors
When it went out from the womb, bursting forth;
[9]When I made a cloud its garment,
And thick darkness its swaddling bands,
[10]And I placed boundaries on it
And set a bolt and doors,
[11]And I said, 'As far as this point you shall come, but no farther;
And here your proud waves shall stop'?

[12]"Have you ever in your life commanded the morning,
And made the dawn know its place,
[13]So that it would take hold of the ends of the earth,
And the wicked would be shaken off from it?
[14]It is changed like clay under the seal;
And they stand out like a garment.
[15]Their light is withheld from the wicked,
And the uplifted arm is broken.

[16]"Have you entered the springs of the sea,
And walked in the depth of the ocean?

[17]Have the gates of death been revealed to you,
And have you seen the gates of deep darkness?
[18]Have you understood the expanse of the earth?
Tell Me, if you know all this.
[19]"Where is the way to the dwelling of light?
And darkness, where is its place,
[20]That you would take it to its territory,
And discern the paths to its home?
[21]You know, for you were born then,
And the number of your days is great!
[22]Have you entered the storehouses of the snow,
And have you seen the storehouses of the hail,
[23]Which I have reserved for a time of distress,
For a day of war and battle?

[24]Where is the way that the light is divided,
And the east wind scattered on the earth?
[25]"Who has split open a channel for the flood,
And a way for the thunderbolt,
[26]To bring rain on a land without people,
On a desert without a person in it,
[27]To satisfy the waste and desolate land,
And to make the seeds of grass to sprout?
[28]Does the rain have a father?
Or who has fathered the drops of dew?
[29]From whose womb has come the ice?
And the frost of heaven, who has given it birth?
[30]Water becomes hard like stone,
And the surface of the deep is imprisoned.

31"Can you tie up the chains of the Pleiades,
Or untie the cords of Orion?
32Can you bring out a constellation in its season,
And guide the Bear with her satellites?
33Do you know the ordinances of the heavens,
Or do you establish their rule over the earth?
34"Can you raise your voice to the clouds,
So that an abundance of water will cover you?
35Can you send flashes of lightning, so that they may go
And say to you, 'Here we are'?

36Who has put wisdom in the innermost being,
Or given understanding to the mind?
37Who can count the clouds by wisdom,
And pour out the water jars of the heavens,
38When the dust hardens into a mass
And the clods stick together?

39"Can you hunt the prey for the lioness,
Or satisfy the appetite of young lions,
40When they crouch in their hiding places,
And lie in wait in their lair?
41Who prepares feed for the raven
When its young cry to God,
And wander about without food?" (NASB)

Um. Hmmmmm. Um. The next four chapters of Job are all like this. I highly implore you to go read them. Speechless. Awe-inspiring. Humbling. God sets his majesty laid out like mastery before Job. God sets a firm boundary for Job. Job is wise to respond the way he did in 42: 1–6:

> [1]Then Job answered the Lord and said,
> [2]"I know that You can do all things,
> And that no plan is impossible for You.
> [3]'Who is this who conceals advice without knowledge?'
> Therefore I have declared that which I did not understand,
> Things too wonderful for me, which I do not know.
> [4]'Please listen, and I will speak;
> I will ask You, and You instruct me.'
> [5]I have heard of You by the hearing of the ear;
> But now my eye sees You;
> [6]Therefore I retract,
> And I repent, sitting on dust and ashes." (NASB)

Did you notice how many boundaries for creation God acknowledged in his laying out of creation and wisdom? The boundaries of the waves, setting measurements of the sky, and commanding the morning are amazing powerful boundaries that belong to God alone. We are familiar with boundaries, but letting go of control is much harder on us than we often like to admit. If we can control it, we can understand it and that makes us feel safe. But just like Job found out with all these marvelous wonders that he doesn't have control, you and I don't have control over much either. The Serenity Prayer, used in Alcoholics Anonymous, begins with accepting what we cannot change, courage to change the things we can, and the wisdom to know the difference. The concepts of accepting, having courage, and wisdom are beginning stages to our knowledge of how little control we have. We only have control over ourselves. We can only change ourselves. We can only set boundaries for ourselves. We must let God do his divine work and be God . . . without us.

Actionable Items:

* You are not God. Release yourself of that responsibility by praying every day for God to teach you how to let go of what you can't control.
* List three things in this scripture from Job that inspire you.
* Can you relate to Job? Pray Job's response every day for the next 30 days. Write down how God responds to you.

Visit my website for prayers and calendars to support you in your journey!

Part 2:

Putting boundaries in place

Chapter 7

Control is an Illusion

Control. This is a word that is probably your best friend, but you may not even recognize it. It sounds . . . abrasive. Rude. Like what other people do. But we all control our environments in many ways. We control whether we keep a clean house or not. We control whether we parent our children or not. We control whether we eat well or not. Every single step in our life is a form of control. So using these examples, how is the "or not" control? You can control things by not doing things (omission) as well as doing things (commission).

You can't control whether someone lives or dies. You can't control whether someone raises their children properly. You can't control who someone marries or divorces. You can't control other people. You can't control what culture does. You can't control how your neighbor behaves. What does this have to do with boundaries? As long as you are trying to control someone else, neither you nor they can have healthy boundaries. You cross their boundary line when you are controlling them, especially when it creates fear in the depth of their heart. You can't make a boundary that you aren't holding, so whenever your control is flared up, there is no boundary line available.

So in order to start establishing boundaries, you must first stop controlling others. There are two basic kinds of unhealthy control: passive control and direct control.

Passive control

Controlling by not doing things is a passive form of control. It is almost more manipulative than direct control because it seems indifferent, lazy. But it is still control, as there are still consequences to our passive actions. For example, we have a choice whether we put a bacon cheeseburger in our mouth or strawberries. We get to control what is put in our mouths as an adult. If we know that we shouldn't be eating a bacon cheeseburger but we choose to anyway, we have just passively controlled the situation. We *chose* to do the easy thing instead of the harder or more disciplined thing. Not paying the bills if it's your responsibility, losing jobs over and over and not helping with household finances, not cleaning up things around the house that need to be done and that you are capable of doing are all examples of passive control by *not* doing something.

Children do not have this same form of control. They are completely vulnerable to what they are given. You can see when children have passively controlling parents, they are out of control and usually miserable for everyone around them, including their passive parents. It is important for parents to embrace the control that comes along with the responsibility of parenting. Parenting is the ultimate form of control and relinquishing it can be one of the greatest challenges for parents. When parents aren't able to release the control at the natural time and natural progression, this is when codependency has a chance of settling in.

Passive control leads to manipulation to get your way. For example, you don't tell your children what to do but tell them, "If you will _____, then I will _____." Fill in those blanks with whatever you want. "If you behave, then I will buy you a treat" is passive control and manipulation. You are telling your child that if they do what you want, you will do what they want. This may seem like "friendly" parenting, but it is passive control. You are the authority. You don't *have* to negotiate with your child. They should do what you tell them to honor your position as their parent. It is your responsibility to teach them the skill of respecting authority. With authority comes boundaries, and children will feel safer if parents set boundaries for them to understand *who* is in control. They inherently know that they are not able to control their environment, their choices, their lives, so when you give them control that is not supposed to be theirs, it will cause misbehavior out of the feeling of being unsafe and not knowing what is dependable.

Strong-willed children are harder to get in line at times, but you can use that to your advantage. This isn't a parenting book, so I will refrain from going down that road, but I want you to know that as a parent it *is* your responsibility to be in control and not to be passive. Your passivity may lead you down a road that will make your life hell for the majority of the rest of your life. Eighteen years of committing and doing that hard part of parenting and holding your boundaries will pay off in many, many years of happy non-direct parenting for the rest of your life, regardless of your kids' decisions. There are many good parenting books. Find one and hold your boundaries and then be deliberate in your actions.

What if the person is an equal? How can someone passively control an equal? Have you been married? We most commonly passively control in marriage. Our spouses are our equals. The man is the head (1 Corinthians 11:3) and leader and the woman is his main sidekick that is critical in every way. The Bible says women are the glory of men (1 Corinthians 11:7); this means that we are a concentrated form of the man. As the book *Eve in Exile* by Rebecca Merkle puts it, "If men are the beer, women are the whiskey." I love that analogy! Women and men are equal in importance with different roles to fulfill the fullness of God's purpose. But that rascally spouse won't do what we want, so we try to control it. Passive control in a marriage can take many forms. It might be the spouse that refuses to have sex. The other spouse will do things to try to make the other spouse interested or beg and plead. The spouse that is refusing to have sex with the other is passively controlling. They are controlling by just *not* doing. Our spouses are the only place we can fulfill our sexual desire, and when one is controlling with the lack of sex, it can be detrimental to the other spouse.

Another form of passive control in marriage is to purchase items and hide them from your spouse. The only reason you hide anything is not to have to answer for it. If hiding things is a must, your marriage lacks communication and boundaries. Usually fear is the reason that we hide things, but sometimes it is just to get what we want. This is a form of manipulation.

Passive control can be detrimental to those around us because we have manipulated them mentally or emotionally, typically to get what we want. Passive control can lead to high codependency because there are no boundaries. If we use manipulation to get what we want, instead of being direct about our needs, feelings, and desires, we hurt our relationships with those around us.

Are you guilty of passive control? Do you recognize that you use manipulation to get what you want from others around you? Pray this prayer with me to help begin the process of breaking the forms of passive control in your life.

Father God,
I have never recognized that I use manipulation to control people around me until today. I need your wisdom and guidance to break those chains for me. Thank you for being intimate with me and loving me so much that you will work with me to change the direction of my thinking. Thank you for giving us the power in the Holy Spirit to overcome areas that are a struggle. I am strong because of you. Open my eyes to see where I am being passively controlled. Prompt my spirit and alert me when I attempt to passively control others. You promise that you do not give us a spirit of fear, but of peace, love, and sound mind. I ask that you heal me from my fear of rejection so I can express my needs directly and can set healthy boundaries around my needs.
In Jesus' name
Amen

Direct control

Direct control is entirely different from passive control. While it doesn't have to be loud and overbearing, you have created fear in the other person. Sometimes physical harm is involved so the other person involved recognizes an actual threat. However, you can be directly controlling without physical abuse. There are plenty of verbal and non-verbal cues that warn the other person that they are pushing it. Direct control doesn't always look like abuse. Sometimes it can look like the person is well-loved and cared for, but in reality, the controlled person on the inside lives in fear. Direct control is always about the person fearing they will lose control. If there is anything they can't predict or prevent, then anger rages. There is basically no grace or mercy in this type of control. It is suffocating for everyone who is being crushed underneath it.

Direct control in a parent/child relationship can be somewhat hard to see because it may look like good parenting. The child may be dressed impeccably and always have every single thing right. From the outside looking in, this seems like wonderful care from the parents, but the child is terrified on the inside to get anything wrong or to have anything out of place because the parent will surely come down on the child. The motivations behind the parenting are about control, not leading, mentoring, and modeling for the child.

Direct control with a spouse might sound like verbal abuse. For example, a woman may say to her man, "You are worthless at everything you do, and you'd be nothing without me!" A man may say to his woman, "If you were worth anything, our house would look better." The need in the first example is that the woman feels uncared for. Instead of being vulnerable and allowing that vulnerability to show, it is easier to tear him down and try to have direct control. She has most likely taken control of everything in the house from finances to kids to all other aspects and now she resents that her "worthless" husband isn't stepping up to the plate. In reality, he is being crushed underneath her control and can't figure out how to move, so he stays very, very still. In the second example, the need is for the man's house to be more orderly. Instead of sharing his need, he uses insults to diminish and demean his wife. The wife, needing love and support from her husband, is crushed by his lack of kindness and vulnerability. She struggles with basic functioning and keeping the house clean is overwhelming.

In both of these examples, the spouse uses direct control to keep from being vulnerable and sharing their needs. If the directly controlling spouse would drop their defenses, which stem from a fear of rejection and fear of not controlling the things and people around them, they would free their other spouse up to meet those needs.

Letting go of control

Again, in order to establish boundaries in a relationship, you first have to let go of any type of control you use over the other person.

I, personally, struggle with direct control more than the passive kind—although I am sure that I have done both forms over the years to make sure that I get my way. Hey, I'm the baby of the family, I like to get my way! I told you, I've spent my entire adult life trying to learn these concepts of boundaries. I don't like being out of control. I don't like feeling like I may be vulnerable to others to be abused or taken advantage of in any way. I have had to learn the areas that I *do* have control over and let go of the areas that I *don't* have control over. I had to lay them at the foot of the cross and know that God can do so much more than I ever imagined (Ephesians 3:20). Letting go was freeing. Scary, yes. I did not master letting anything go overnight. I just kept making the next right step. I would have to dialog with myself. It might look something like this:

Issue: Your husband didn't throw away his food wrappers from dinner last night when you asked him to. You wake up the next day, and lo and behold, they are still on the kitchen table.

This may seem trivial, but remember we are talking about direct control people. It can be something simple that sets all the control off. In that situation, you have two choices: go into direct control mode, tearing him down and ripping into him and crushing him under the weight of your words; or pick up the wrappers, throw them away, keep your mouth shut, and *let it go!* Those three words are the critical part: *let it go*. See, if you choose to stew on the fact that he didn't throw his wrappers away and then torture him later in another fight about it, you still have been holding onto control, just diverted control.

You may be a passive-aggressive direct controller. Maybe you just wouldn't have talked to him for a week . . . maybe two. You would let him "sit and think about what he did," but most likely he already felt remorse once he realized his mistake or he's so confused about why you won't talk to him *now*. Since you have given him the silent treatment so many times before, he doesn't quite know why anymore. Yet, he still knows he is paying for something ("she's mad about somethin' . . ." shrugs shoulders and picks up the remote control).

Whether you use direct control, diverted control, or passive-aggressive direct control, in your heart, you were going to make him "pay" for not doing what you wanted him to do. That is not the heart of a believer. A healthy believer in Jesus knows that He was the ultimate propitiation for our sins (1 John 2:2). We controllers and those whom we are trying to control do not have to atone for our actions and behaviors through abuse.

When we feel the need to make someone pay for something, we haven't set healthy boundaries for ourselves or let them know where our boundaries are. Making them pay is our way of vindicating their "wrong" in our minds. It is usually very hurtful to the person on the other side. I still have to walk through thinking processes at times, especially if I am angry about a situation. My anger will often propel my direct control, and I have to choose not to act, think, or behave through a negative, hurtful mindset. The Holy Spirit gives me the power to do this. It is not just because I am some super awesome human that has overcome my flaws; quite the contrary, even in my mess, the Holy Spirit works with me and through me to give me a sound mind, love, peace, and the biggest two, *grace* and *mercy*.

Grace and mercy are the breakers of all control. These are the mark of God on all Christians. Grace tells us that we have the freely given unmerited love of God, which we extend to others, and mercy says that we deserve to be punished but instead we are forgiven fully. But when we establish direct control, we are not allowing grace and mercy to be active in our lives.

Physical abuse of a spouse or children, not allowing others to have failures, and stepping on another's toes to make something happen that is their responsibility are all examples of direct control. If you find that you struggle with direct control, pray this prayer with me.

Lord Jesus,
I am guilty of direct control. My spirit is willing, but my flesh is
weak. Thank you, Lord, for your never-ending love. Thank you for
dying on the cross and completing the work for me that I cannot do
on my own. I think I have control over things, but I don't. I need you
to teach me how to rest in your divinity and that I don't have to be
in control of others. I am OK because I have you. You are able to do
exceedingly and abundantly more than I can ever imagine, and I
am thankful for that. Forgive me for hurting and harming others
with my controlling tendencies. I recognize that it comes from a place
of fear, and I am going to rest my fear at the foot of the cross. I will
destroy my life with the need to control others to keep myself in a false
sense of safety. Reveal to me areas that I want to control the most so
I can learn to resolve it. Open my eyes to your ways, God, that I may
be able to honor you with my life.
In Jesus' name
Amen

Life is too short and way too long for us to live in a state of trying to
control things that are out of our control. We can spend our lives
in misery and in a state of torture because we never set boundaries
that are healthy and never let anyone know where our boundaries
are, or we can begin today to enjoy life and set healthy boundaries
for ourselves. We can learn to let go of things we can't control. We
can break away from being codependent on others and realize that
we can't live their lives for them.

Now when it comes to minor children, it may seem like you are
"controlling" them to do what you want them to do, but really you
are the authority and can and should set clear boundaries. They are

under your care so you do need them to do what you want them to do. As I stated before, it is your responsibility and duty to teach them to have a healthy respect for authority. Remember, rules without relationship leads to rebellion. But you need to establish rules through boundaries, not through control.

Make sure that your relationship with your children is being fed strongly so that as you set rules, your children will have a desire to meet you there. It may look different for every child. I have five children, and you better believe how I do things with each one varies. It is similar enough that they know what to expect overall, but each child needs something different. Invest in your children when they are young so you feel comfortable with them spreading their wings as teens. You will be able to let them do so without fear. When I say without fear, I mean that you have done the hard work of learning to let go and so can trust that they can and will do the right thing. You taught them to. As long as your children are teens, their boundaries and yours intersect. They should be able to have a certain level of responsibility and freedom but never without accountability.

Your parenting should always be propelled out of love, which is the motivation for boundaries, and not just obedience out of fear, which is the motivation of control. Fear is a powerful propeller, but it is also a destroyer, and if you raise your child by fear, they have a greater chance of becoming a nightmare or just incapable of standing on their own two feet. When you lead and guide your children, talk to them about boundaries. By having firm boundaries in your house, they will understand the concept. Bedtime, meal time, mom and dad time are all examples of boundaries that you may have already in your home. Talk to your kids about how and why these are boundaries.

My youngest two daughters are super rascally at bedtime. They have bunk beds and love to chit-chat at night, and sometimes that can mean they stay up well past their bedtime. So I will tell them, "I am putting you to bed. This is your boundary. If you cross this boundary, you will not be able to play on screens tomorrow. Please honor this time and lie down and close your eyes and go to bed." Sometimes this works, and sometimes it doesn't. However, if it does not work, the next day they will certainly lose their opportunity to play on screens. They chose to have consequences instead of honoring the boundary. That's OK. Sometimes that is exactly how it will work with people.

Boundaries versus control

If you set boundaries in the hope to control/manipulate others into doing what you want, you have completely lost the purpose of boundaries. Boundaries *are not* for you to control others. They are for your safety. They set the line on what you can handle. Say your child is a drug addict and you have bailed him/her out of jail numerous times and now you have set a boundary. You surely know that you can't control whether they use drugs or not, but you can establish a boundary to state how involved you are with that experience. Boundaries would include: telling them you won't bail them out of jail; or you can tell them they aren't allowed over unless they go to rehab. Each of these statements explain what you can handle for your safety. There isn't any recognition about their behavior. Attempting to control the situation would be if you allow them over and then badger them the entire time for being high. You knew they were using but you didn't protect yourself from being affected by it.

You can count on the fact that there are consequences for boundaries being established, so be prepared and better yet, make an effort to get support, especially if you are dealing with a drug-addict child. You will need so much help to hold those lines when your parent's heart is struggling to see the benefit of boundaries. Consequences may include: a person no longer talking to you, rage from the addict/alcoholic/abusive relationship, withdrawal from a close friend, or isolation from family if they are unhealthy for you to be near or involved.

Life is too short and yet way too long not to hold boundaries that keep you safe.

Actionable Items:

- Learn your controlling tendency. Take the quiz on my website www.believinginboundaries.com.
- Make a list of five practical ways you can change your habits that make you feel that you are in control.
- List three relationships that could be improved by establishing boundaries. Work with one relationship at a time. One boundary at a time.

Visit my website for a quiz and more information.

Chapter 8

Art of Forgiveness—Freedom for Everyone

Forgiveness, and the power that it holds, is one of the most confusing and misunderstood principles that we have in Christianity. Boundaries and forgiveness are like brand-new lovers. They go hand in hand. Forgiveness for others, forgiveness for ourselves, forgiveness for God, forgiveness for all. Forgiveness is a power for the one doing the forgiving. It releases you and those around you from having to account for what is happening. Forgiveness is the epitome of letting go. Forgiveness is ultimate trust in God. Forgiveness is the full acceptance of the work of Jesus Christ on the cross.

What is forgiveness?

According to Dictionary.com, forgive means to grant pardon for or remission of (an offense, debt, etc); absolve, to give up all claim on account of, remit (debt, obligation, etc.), to grant pardon to (a person), to cease to feel resentment against, to cancel an indebtedness or liability of. Can you see how forgiving those around you, yourself, and God can be the most powerful thing in your life? Let forgiveness bring along its friend, boundaries, and you will have so much freedom for yourself and those around you. Your level of offendedness will be gone. You will be able to breathe and rest.

To understand forgiveness, let's meet Jesus in the Garden of Gethsemane (Luke 22:39–71). Before we start this part of his story, I'll give you a little background. Jesus taught in the temples and on mountainsides and really every opportunity He had. What He taught expanded on and challenged everything the Jewish people had believed for generations and generations. He told them crazy things like, "If you hate in your heart, you have committed murder," and "If you lust in your heart after another, you have committed adultery." He chastised the most religious in his day and called them vipers and white-washed tombs. He insulted all their well-meaning stances. He loved people no one else would have anything to do with. He called a bunch of men, men that were vagabonds and not well-liked, to follow him closely and learn everything so they would build his church (Matthew 16:18). Needless to say, the religious leaders of the day hated Jesus. This is where we meet him in the Garden.

Jesus has some of his disciples with him. He is basically asking them to hang out with him and pray with him. He knew his time was coming to face the cross and that he would have to love the world with all the depths of his divinity. Like typical friends, who don't know the desperate thing happening in His life, they kept falling asleep on Jesus. He kept waking his friends and implored them to pray for him. Still, they slept, not knowing what was around the corner for their beloved leader. Judas, one of Jesus' disciples, was the catalyst for Jesus' arrest. He betrayed the Son of God for some money. Jesus knew that Judas would betray him, but the night before this situation, Jesus sat at the table with Judas and made a covenant with him. Despite knowing that Judas' heart was against him, He chose to let him remain at the table. Jesus knew that this betrayal was in God's plan, though it did not hurt less because of that.

Judas and the Roman guards showed up in the Garden, taking everyone but Jesus by surprise. He gave himself up. One more time, the Son of God *gave* himself up. This is just the beginning of the gift of the cross for us and teaching us the art of forgiveness. Jesus could have defended himself. He had all of heaven at his disposal and could have called down warring angels. He could have killed every single one of those people on the spot, but in His love and grace and mercy and forgiveness power, He gave himself. Jesus came for this moment.

How does this look like a boundary? Jesus came to tear the veil and break the boundary that sin had created between God and us, his children. We have a seriously bad codependent relationship with sin. We do the very thing we don't want to do. But we are propelled to do it because of sin inside of us (Romans 7:14–25). When the fruit of the Tree of Knowledge of Good and Evil was eaten, we opened the entire human experience to be sick with this knowledge, but Jesus came to restore, giving us life and to have it in abundance (John 10:10). God wanted us to have the power to overcome sin in our life and the power of forgiveness for our freedom.

When Jesus was on the cross on Golgotha, He said, "Forgive them Father; for they do not know what they are doing" (Luke

23:34). Jesus, dying a horrid death, plead for forgiveness for us! The Bible says that he was beaten beyond recognition (Isaiah 50:6, 52:14), yet he was pleading for God to forgive. Why? Because freedom. Forgiveness brings freedom.

Forgiveness with boundaries

When we follow Christ's example of forgiveness, we release others. We absolve them of what we think they owe us. If you are codependent with an addicted family member, you may think that you are owed an explanation on why he/she stole from you. The answer is because the person is sick with addiction. You already know the answer, but you want an explanation. Something to make it better . . . something to make it make sense. It will never make sense because addiction behaviors are a corruption of the person. So how do we forgive that? You have to let God do it through you. You do not have the power in yourself to let go of the devastating things that people do to you, especially when you are in unhealthy relationships. But since forgiveness is the key to holding your boundary without letting the cruel and unkind things that are said offend you, you must invite God to help you. There is freedom for you and those in relationships with you when forgiveness is possible.

Jesus absolved Judas' betrayal while He was on the cross. Jesus knew that Judas was not intentionally hurting Jesus just to hurt Him. Judas did what he had to do for his own gain. So Jesus was able to remove the need to control Judas. Even though Jesus offers forgiveness in full all the time, sometimes, we don't accept it and, therefore, do not understand that it is for our good. Why do we not accept it? It's free! It's good! It's an amazing gift!!

We don't accept it because it comes with the boundary of repentance. The boundary of forgiveness in healthy relationships is repentance. Repentance is an acknowledgement of what we did wrong and then an active movement in the opposite direction. God gives us forgiveness within the boundary of repentance. We must first repent.

Just like God had a boundary for forgiveness, we need a boundary when we forgive. Forgiveness is a powerful tool to offer freedom, but it is not meant to make you a doormat. Yet, the Bible says to forgive over and over again. True. In Matthew, Jesus and Peter are having a conversation and Peter asks Jesus, "Lord, how often will my brother sin against me, and I forgive him? As many as seven times?" Jesus said to him, "I do not say to you seven times, but seventy times seven." My friends, when you take this one part out of the context of the entirety of scripture that surrounds it, you have led yourself into a dangerous place to be deceived. This scripture is not the open door to being a doormat.

If you are using the Bible as an excuse to allow yourself to be mistreated and abused and even in some cases tortured. STOP. RIGHT. NOW. That is not the heart of the Father, and scripture is meant to be a light unto our path (Psalm 119:105), not a shackle around our feet.

Let's back up a few verses before this one passage of scripture that is often misstated. In Matthew 18:15–18, Jesus is talking about when a person sins against us, we are to "go and show him his fault in private; if he listens to you, you have won your brother. But if he does not listen to you, take one or two more people with you, so that by the mouth of two or three witnesses, every fact may be confirmed" (NASB 1995, Bible.com). This is the call to repentance. This is the moment that the person that has sinned against you has the opportunity to recognize his/her folly and change the behavior. The call to repentance is the first action to the gift of forgiveness.

It is after this word from Jesus that He tells Peter that he is to forgive over and over again. People will hurt us! People will disappoint us. People will seem like the enemy sometimes, but they are not the enemy (Ephesians 6:10). Forgiving over and over and over in healthy relationships offers the freedom for both people in that relationship to make mistakes and repent and forgive freely. This pattern creates a healthy relationship with people. Just like how God freely gives us forgiveness and freedom through the work of the cross, but it requires that we recognize our folly and change our direction of thinking and behaviors. We change what we are doing, not to earn forgiveness, but because we recognize that we cannot be in a healthy relationship and hurt the other person.

However, if you are in a relationship that is not reciprocal and the person doesn't acknowledge or recognize how their behavior has hurt you or affected you, this is not the place for forgiveness with connection. Remember earlier in this book when we talked about creation and its boundaries. You may have to become like the sky is with the water. You may stay connected (e.g., with a child or parent or spouse), but you can separate and put space between you to keep yourself safe. This space may be physical, but it can also be mental and emotional.

If you are with someone who isn't physically harmful but is mentally and emotionally draining, a little physical space for a period of time may be helpful for you to get your head clear. Often when you are in the storm of a relationship, it is hard to see clearly.

The more clearly you can think and see, the more you'll be able to set and hold your boundaries. If you cannot physically separate, then begin to get an accountability group to help you. Find people who have been in your situation to help shine light in areas that you can't see for yourself.

If someone is physically harming you, leave or separate immediately. Find a safe home or somewhere to help you. Physical harm is never OK. God will never justify someone being physically abusive to you. The national hotline number for physical abuse is 1–800–799-SAFE (7233).

Matthew 6:14–15 tells us that if we forgive our brothers, then God will forgive us, but if we do not forgive our brothers, then God will not forgive us. This scripture never says that we have to continue in an unhealthy relationship. See, forgiveness is something that happens inside of you. It has nothing to do with the other person. Well, it will change the way you treat the other person, but it has nothing to do with them being an active part of forgiveness. For example, you can forgive someone who has sexually molested you, but you shouldn't ever have anything to do with that person again. Forgiving them releases you from carrying the burden of what they did to you. Forgiveness does not justify what they did. Forgiveness never says it's OK. Forgiveness says, "I trust that God is big enough and loves me enough to do what He will with this action and behavior. I have no control over this situation or what happened to me, so I am going to let my Father handle it."

Forgiveness is for your heart to release the weight of sin that it can't account for, and if it was something done to you, it wasn't yours to carry. When we are violated, it can be very, very, very hard to let the hurt go because we feel somehow that if we hold onto it, we will make them pay. The other person will somehow feel convicted or punished by us if we hang onto the anger and offense. They won't. Often, people don't care that they hurt others because they are operating out of their own brokenness, in the same ways in which they were hurt. Unforgiveness mostly just hurts you and your heart. I heard a saying once that "unforgiveness is much like setting yourself on fire hoping the other person gets burned." That may be a harsh analogy, but I can appreciate its point. If we harm ourselves hoping someone else might get burned, are we really making the point?

Forgiving God

At the beginning of this chapter, I stated that you have to forgive God, and I want to expound on that a little. When I have said that to people, their eyebrows raise with confusion. "How can *you* forgive God?!" is the resounding look on their faces. Well, free will is the freedom that God gave us that differentiates us from the rest of creation. It isn't the only difference, but one of the most powerful. We speak because God spoke, we can build and settle nations and cities, we can use logic and reason, and we have opposable thumbs. Thank you, God! But free will. That sucker is the place that can get us in the most trouble. Free will is what allows us to feel that there is no God or that He is here to serve us. Free will is the absolute freedom to feel, think, act and believe however we want, including lack of forgiveness towards God. Yet, free will also has its boundaries *if* we are to have a good relationship with our Father.

Relationship is everything; the relationship with our family members, friends, church members, coworkers and especially, God. These relationships are the building of our life. The people that remember us when we are gone and God, who we will face after we are dead, are the relationships that matter. We will answer for all the things done in secret and all the things that we are sorry for.

People often question why and how we can forgive God. But, yes, it is necessary to forgive God. When we are hurt, who do we usually blame? God.

- "Why did God let this happen to me?"
- "Why did God allow that person in my life?"
- "Why was I born into this family, God?"
- "Why did my husband/baby/mother/father die?"
- "Why is my son/daughter a drug addict?"
- "Why is my husband/wife so mean?"

There are so many questions we ask God. If you want the answer, you can go read the same answer over again that He gave Job. The answer is, He doesn't have to account for his majesty. God is not for us, but we are for Him. He is the Creator and Father, and outside of that, He owes us nothing.

When we are angry at God for things that are indeed very unfair in life, it is important that we forgive Him. Not because God *needs* our forgiveness, but because we need it. We need to release the weight off of our heart so that God can freely work with us. When we shut him out over an offense, we lose our ability to have a right relationship with God. When we harbor an offense against Him, we are saying that we have the ability to judge His actions and that

He is to account to us. This is wrong. This is dangerous ground. This is not going to get you what you long for.

When my husband died and I had five very young kids, a business to run, and homeschool to teach, I was incredibly angry. I was called into this marriage for what?? To be left completely hanging?? I was devastated. I couldn't find two brain cells to rub together. In grace, when you face that kind of loss, your brain shuts down so you don't buckle under the weight of devastation. However, I needed all my brain cells and couldn't find any. I was so very angry at God. I couldn't figure out why he did that to me. Why did my kids have to lose their dad like I did as a kid? Oh! I knew the devastation of losing a father at a young age. I became a widow at the same age that my mom became a widow. It seemed so very cruel. I felt like God was playing a game with my family and me. I felt angry all the time. Betrayed. Let down. Bitterness was creeping in. Though I could feel God right there with me, my heart was in complete wreckage. It took every single ounce of the studying of the Bible, learning of God, and building my relationship with God that I had done the decade before to not just completely turn my back on God and say forget it! Every. Single. Ounce.

I had to actively work through forgiveness toward God. I had to come to terms that God wasn't doing anything *to* me. He wasn't being a mean cruel God that was using my life like a chess piece. He is a loving Father that sees the things I can't see, and He can use things in my life for good (Jeremiah 29:11) if I let him, even the hard things. I had to allow forgiveness to say, "I trust that God is big enough and loves me enough to do what He will with this action and behavior. I have no control over this situation or what happened to me, so I am going to let my Father handle it."

Releasing wasn't easy. It didn't happen overnight. I had to realize within myself *who* I was even mad at. Realizing that I was indeed angry with God and, now, had to forgive Him and that He would give me that power to do so was a lightbulb moment for me. Because He is such a loving Father, He walked me through the journey of forgiving Him and trusting Him. He will do the same for you. If you are struggling with forgiving humans in your life, maybe sit back and look to see how angry you are with God. You may need to start with forgiveness for God so He is free to help you along with forgiveness in your human relationships. He will give you the ability to forgive Him because He loves you and knows that forgiveness is for us. Unlike the forgiveness with humans, there is no call to repentance for God. So you are free to openly forgive him as often and as much as you need to. Usually, the reason we feel the need to forgive God is not that He actually did something wrong to us, but more because we feel angry about something that someone else did to us. But since we are image-bearers of God, when someone hurts us, God often gets blamed for the sin in that person's life. To be clear, God cannot and will not sin against you. God is holy and we are here for His glory. God didn't *cause* anything bad or wrong to happen to you because He is a loving Father. The bad or wrong thing that happened came because of sin in this world. Death is a product of sin. Abuses of all kinds are a product of sin. Abuse and all evil things are divvied out by the enemy of our souls, Satan.

Jesus came to redeem those things, and that comes from the heart of a loving Father. He created safety and healing for us. But we often blame Him instead of Satan. Sometimes when children suffer great sadnesses as a child and one parent leaves, the other parent "pays" for the sadness of the child. In counseling, they call it deferred anger. So the parent the child is actually angry at isn't around to have the consequences of the anger, so the parent that is still around gets the brunt of the anger. It can seem so unfair to the parent that is still there. He/she is the supportive parent. He/she is the parent that has sacrificed and been available, yet he/she is the one that gets all the heartache the sad child can dish out. This isn't an exact comparison since Satan isn't a parent figure for us, but it is similar. Satan corrupts from the back door. He uses the sneaky sides to wreck us, and then all we have is God to blame because He is faithful and beside us. God is recognized, while Satan is just looming in the background hoping to go unseen. He knows that if he can corrupt your heart against God, then he can move in and wreck so much more of you and your children, your legacy, and your generations who come after you.

Forgiveness rips open the veil across your heart and allows light to come in and to restore what was formerly broken. Forgiveness breaks chains off us! Forgiveness makes us so free that we are able to love and hold boundaries and be strong without having to worry about how to solve things we have no control over. Forgive for freedom's sake.

Actionable Items:

- What are three relationships that I have struggled with forgiveness?
- What three areas of my life do I need to work on forgiveness toward God?
- Work through your forgiveness using one or more of these practical ways:

- Pray daily
- Make reminder cards and place them around your house
- Talk to the person with whom you need to work forgiveness out and begin steps to healing

(Note: If three is too many to start with, by all means, start with one. Sometimes we have some really damaged relationships, and we can only handle one at a time. That is OK. Start with the first person and then move to the next when you are ready. If you can list ten off of your head at the beginning, take the top three and stop there. Once you have worked on those three relationships, then you can make a list of three more. Don't try to do too much at once because you may become overwhelmed. Remember, boundaries will begin to change and shift the relationships, so you will need to take it slowly.)

Chapter 9

Freedom Doesn't Mean a-free-for-All

I know I'm not the only one that feels like this modern culture has drastically flipped on its head. In America, we have so many freedoms, and we have taken great liberty with the boundaries that keep stability within a culture. It seems like we get messages from every direction telling us to do whatever feels good to us. We are bombarded with faux ideas of self-care and self-love, yet they always seem to leave us empty. We long for more. More safety. More control. More belonging.

As I write this, we are in the Covid-19 pandemic. The mandates are to wear masks and stay at least six feet from others. There is a constant sense of fear and a feeling that death is imminent. Yet there are no real boundaries around what is truly safe and what isn't. We want to control. We want freedom, but only if it means we have control. Are we able to see that God is in control? Are we able to trust him with ourselves? Our kids? Our finances? Our futures?

I am answering that with a resounding no. We also have our culture trying to push God out and change His boundaries. Our culture can sway us, but we need to draw a boundary with how much we will listen and let culture influence us.

Believer, you need to fight your tendencies with everything you have and not let the culture mold you but allow God and His Word to set your culture and your boundaries. Cultural boundaries can be difficult to establish without the Bible leading you. You may question everything you've ever known. Questioning is good. Questioning opens a conversation to be had that can open you up to possibilities that you haven't thought of before. When you have those questions, turn to the Bible, as it is the only truth that can be absolutely counted on for sound thinking and following God's way. We try to make Him fit our ways to soften the truth because we don't like some of His boundaries, but we only fool ourselves when we do this.

Seeking God's perspective on all of these topics is the most important thing you can do. I can't possibly cover them all, but I do want to touch on some of the hot topics of the current cultural climate and speak to them from a biblical perspective because setting your boundaries around these topics and many others is important and challenging. You will get backlash from the culture because it will go against what they are saying and wanting. It was the same in Jesus' day.

Behold, I send you out as sheep in the midst of wolves; so be shrewd as serpents and innocent as doves. But be aware of men for they will hand you over to the courts and scourge you in their synagogues; and you will be brought before governors and kings for my sake, as a testimony to them and to the Gentiles. But when they hand you over, do not worry about how or what you are to say; for it will be given you in that hour what to say. For it is not you who speak, but it is the Spirit of your Father who speaks in you. Brother will betray brother to death, and father his child; and children will rise up against parents and cause them to be put to death. **You will be hated because of My name,** *but it is the one who has endured to the end who will be saved. (Matthew 10:16–23 NASB)*

If the world hates you, you know that it has hated Me before it hated you. If you were of the world, the world would love its own; but because you are not of the world, the world hates you. (John 15:18–19 NASB)

Jesus was hated because everything he said and spoke countered what they wanted to hear. They didn't want to hear it because we, as humans, are prone to sin. We are a broken vessel that Jesus came to mend. I don't know if you have ever broken a vase that you really loved and tried to put it back together, but it is truly difficult! There are curves, so even if you lay it on its side, it isn't level or flat. Sometimes you have to repair it one or two pieces at a time. You have to slowly and painstakingly rebuild it. After you have completed putting the pieces together over time, it is best to let it stand upright and settle into its repair. If you stand it upright and a piece falls off, then you will have to revisit that piece and attempt again to make it stay in its place.

This is much what we are like in the healing phase of Christianity. We are broken with hurts, traumas, stinkin' thinkin', corrupt ideas, and selfish ambitions. Sin created an unhealthy codependency that needed a healer. Jesus can mend us, but humans can do some serious damage to themselves and others around them when they are in their mending process. You will need to set strong boundaries for your heart not to resist, as you begin to heal, because Jesus is going to counter every single thing you think because it's stinkin' thinkin'. When we are countered in life, we tend to buck it. Jesus was so familiar with this inherent reaction that he warned His followers about it. Jesus tells us because we are not of this world that we will be hated.

I have yet to meet anyone that genuinely likes to be told that they are wrong. Everyone I know gets angry or defensive first. As believers, we have the Holy Spirit to guide us and let us know when we are wrong and how to right the wrong. The world, however, doesn't have that guidance. So there will be many times that when you are countering what they think or believe and say it is wrong, anger will be the first and most persistent response. Boundaries are helpful in how you process the response.

Our culture right now is ripped apart with ultimate division and selfishness. It's a "my way is the only way" culture. Disagreeing with someone doesn't give anyone the right to be mean or unkind to others. Boundaries are meant to help you establish safety for you, not hatred or malice towards anyone. Kindness in establishing boundaries will often go much farther and speak louder. However, if you have a boundary crosser, you may have to be more firm in letting that person know there is a boundary line in place. Scripture sets boundaries into place, whether we like them or not. This is where our heart leans toward God or away from Him. Let's look at what scripture says about some hot topics of today.

Homosexuality/gay marriage

In Genesis 2:24, the Bible says that a man leaves his mother and father and becomes one flesh with his wife. There is no concept of gay marriage anywhere in the Bible. Every reference to marriage is about a man and a woman.

This is one of the hottest and most volatile topics in our current day. God loves people who participate in the homosexual lifestyle and many love God too. This is not a question of salvation or of love. This is a question of how we are designed to be based on God.

Since every reference to marriage is based on man and woman and sex was designed only to be in marriage, then logically, the design for sexuality is for man and woman. The sexual organs are made to fit appropriately and also work together to create a child, which is the physical example of taking two people and creating one. The spiritual law God set into place is that things we see physically begin in the spiritual, develop into the natural, and then end in the spiritual. When a man and a woman come together and make a child, it is an example of that spiritual law. Marriage is not man-made but God-designed, and sex is not man-made, it is also God-designed. So these two practices are spiritual principles we get to enjoy in our lives.

Romans 1:24–32 tells us that God will give us over to desires of "their" or "our" hearts to sexual impurity and degrading our bodies with one another. This means that these are our desires, not

God's desires. If our goal as Christians is just to live for our desires, then we open all sorts of lifestyles and things become open to our interpretation. So this scripture explains at the very beginning that the issue is that we are operating out of self and not out of God. This very issue is at the core of our belief system as a Christian! Are we out for ourselves or are we going to do it God's way? That is the primary question. Following Christ requires sacrifice and dying to our flesh. If we want to follow Christ, we must lay down all of us: our desires and wants and preferences must hang on that cross with Christ.

1 Corinthians 6:9 in the original Greek uses the word *arsenokoites,* which translates as "abuser of oneself with mankind" or "defile oneself with mankind." To abuse and defile ourselves is not the heart of the Father for any area of our lives, especially sexually. Defiling ourselves by giving into the desires of our flesh will ultimately leave us unfulfilled and desiring more because we are designed to be in union with God.

Gender clarity issues

Genesis 1:26 says, "Let us make man in Our image," and verse 27 says, "God created man in His own image, in the image of God he created him; male and female He created them." In verse 26, there is the plural "our" and "us," indicating there is another part to the Godhead. We know God as Father and Jesus as Son, so that only leaves the Holy Spirit to be the female part of the Godhead. The Holy Spirit is what carries life and ushered Jesus here to Earth into Mary. There are only two genders. Male. Female.

They have very powerful roles made in the image of God. You cannot erase the DNA of someone. You can nip, tuck, snip, push, and do whatever you want to the flesh, but you cannot alter the spiritual principle of creation and DNA. You were designed before you were ever on this Earth to fulfill a role and a purpose. You were given the DNA to master the task that you were designed for. Science may be able to visually change the looks, but the design by our Creator cannot be flushed out. We have an intricate structure that speaks to the Creator, and as hard as we may try, I am going to be bold enough to say that it can never ever be erased or altered to be fully changed.

Heart of slavery issues

Interestingly enough, the Bible doesn't seem to be necessarily against slavery as a principle. You will find scriptures speaking to masters and slaves throughout scripture, in both the Old and New Testaments. Ephesians 6:5 and 9, Colossians 4:1, Galatians 3:28, 1 Peter 2:18, and Titus 2:9–10 are some of the New Testament scriptures. So what do we do with this scripture? It is against everything we've been taught. How can God not be boldly against it and say slavery is wrong?

Slavery is a human condition. It doesn't always have to do with race or oppression of a race. When we hold someone indebted to us, we have made a slave out of them. OUCH! How? You may ask. The definition of slavery is anytime we can hold someone captive, and this captivity may come in actual form or just in thoughts and behaviors.

Let's talk about practical tangible slavery first. God is adamant about how to treat someone in another's care. There are still many cultures today that practice slavery for many reasons. Wikipedia says in its article "Slavery in the 21st Century" that an estimated 40+ million people are in slavery. You may not see it in your backyard, but it is happening all around the world. I think God speaking to it is pertinent so that there is a standard by which to be held. Slavery is illegal all over the world, so there is now no regulation for the practice of slavery. All modern-day slavery is practiced without any accountability for the ones doing it and so I think that the Bible continuing to speak toward it keeps it relevant for all of us who believe. We are to be advocates and defenders of those who may be caught in the modern practices.

What about the children? Children are absolutely off-limits to God to be harmed. In Matthew 18:6 and Luke 17:2, we are told it would be better to tie a millstone—these are the large stones used to grind grain—around the neck and be cast into the sea before we corrupt or harm a child. Basically, you'd be better off killing yourself than harming or corrupting a child. Children are innocent and fully dependent on those around them for care. God, and his Father's heart, is very protective of children. Accroding to Wikipedia, it is estimated that around ten million children are in slavery. Some of these children have been born into slavery and it is all that they know.

Now we have the more complex idea of holding someone in slavery by our thoughts and actions, but we don't physically have control over the person. We hold someone to slavery when we think they owe us. Have you ever said, "He/she owes me! I'll make them pay!" This is the heart of an enslaver. You may not physically force them into labor or own them as property, but you might be thinking that you are getting what is owed to you. What about if someone has done something wrong to you and you intend to make them pay by forcing them to do something? Have you helped someone and held them captive when you know they can't pay you back? These are the same heart issues as actual physical slavery. Living in a state of grace and forgiveness removes the idea that someone owes you something, be it money, time, work, or even themselves. Jesus wrecked the Pharisees by telling them that if they hate in their heart, they have committed murder, and if they look at a woman with lust in their eyes, they have committed adultery. These are heart issues just like slavery. So if you hold someone captive and indebted to you, you have held them in slavery to you.

Sometimes it is easy to dislike "them." You know, those other people, who aren't like you. Sometimes it is hard to realize that maybe you are "them."

Premarital sex

Sex was made for the parameters of marriage. Anything other than keeping sex in that design removes God from the picture and is based on our own desires. The practice of living out of our desires over God's will always leave us broken, in sin, and hurting, and there are consequences of these actions that we cannot foresee. Hebrews 13:4 says the marriage bed should be undefiled. It is hard to have an undefiled bed when you bring everyone with you that you have had sex with previously. You cannot erase the attachment that sex brings between two people. There is no amount of time that cancels it or space that makes you forget. God does not want us to be left in pieces. He wants us whole and the more self-control we practice, even though it is dang hard, the better off we will be in the long run for our spouses. Sex is sold to us in our culture as casually pleasurable. It is pleasurable, but when it is casual, the heart always pays the price. It is a steep price for a moment of pleasure. You may not always know the true cost until it is too late and the damage has spread to your marriage and spouse.

<u>Bondage and s&m</u>

There are Christian Grey's out there, and young people are learning more and more at a younger age, so I think this topic should be touched on. B (Bondage), D (Discipline), S(Sadism), M (Masochism) is a sexually erotic practice that can vary greatly depending on the person. Traditionally, Christian cultures aren't comfortable talking about what happens between the sheets, which leaves people with unanswered questions. I am not promoting or discouraging BDSM. I believe Holy Spirit conviction will be critical as your curiosity may grow. I'm going to stick with Hebrews 13:4 for this part because I think it is fitting here as well. The marriage bed is undefiled. So if you and your spouse wanna get a little freaky in the sheets, as long as you are both OK with it and there isn't any fear or condemnation, you are free to enjoy each other. Please know that this kind of lifestyle can be a slippery slope, so I would highly encourage you to bring the Holy Spirit with you at each and every step. If you feel conviction, walk away from it. The Holy Spirit will guide you in your marriage. Not all BDSM is harmful or dangerous or scary, so don't feel like it has to fall into those categories.

However, if you are practicing BDSM in any other form outside of marriage, it would fall under the "fornication" and sin category. Sexual corruption is not biblical. The vulnerability it takes to feel safe with someone to adventure into the world of BDSM shouldn't be found anywhere or with anyone who isn't your spouse and who isn't fully invested in you and your safety.

Pornography

Matthew 5:27–28 gives us a clear picture that pornography is not OK. When you are engaging with porn, you are bringing another person into your sexual experience. Remember, sex was created by God, so it is by His rules that we must safely carry out the fulfillment of sex. The scripture says that if you look at a woman with lust in your eyes, you have committed adultery. Was He leaving the women out here? No! He was talking to a group of men, so He didn't need to specify women in this particular sentence, but nonetheless, the principle remains true for both sexes. If a woman is lusting after another man, she has also committed adultery.

There is no wiggle room here even within the confines of marriage. Porn is never OK. If you and your spouse are watching porn together, you are still inviting someone else and a potentially demonic oppression into your sexual experience. You cannot at any point watch porn and remove fornication and adultery from the equation.

Currently, porn addiction has become one of the leading issues in marriages, causing divorces and division in masses. Men tend to be more subject to this issue because they are visually stimulated by the female form. I also think that is why Jesus told the men that they shouldn't even look at a woman lustfully: men think they can look and as long as they don't touch, they are OK. It isn't so folks. Men, no looking lustfully at other women. God hopefully gifted you with a wife (Proverbs 18:22) that you can look at and enjoy. If you don't have a wife, seek one and pray for one. Hopefully, as you work through this book and learn more about boundaries, you can find a great wife!

Children are a burden issues

Culturally, children have become seen as burdensome. Yes, parenting is a sacrifice. Hopefully, creating boundaries with your kids and family will be so helpful and take the confusion and potential misery out of your experience so that you can sit back and enjoy the fruits of your labor in your children. But kids are important. We shouldn't listen to the culture and instead should build a boundary that having kids is a commandment from God. The Bible, over and over again, tells children to obey and honor their parents. Be the example for your kids by doing that for your parents and teach them how to honor you in all ways.

Parenting is a beautiful gift. It teaches us so much about the heart of our Father God. When I had my first son, it was the first time I understood the depth of the sacrifice that God made with Jesus on the cross. It was the first time I ever thought to myself that I can't imagine the love one must have to sacrifice so much for others and for others who shun and mock and hate God, yet it did not sway Him. Children are part of our legacy that continues, and they are a little piece of our immortality that stays here in the form of genes. Since everything starts in the spirit, plays out in the natural world, and ends in the spirit, having children is a big, important part of that cycle. Our children were created before they were ever knitted together in our wombs (Psalm 139: 13-16), and then once they have lived here on Earth, they will return to their spiritual state and be eternal with us, hopefully in heaven.

Psalm 127:3 says that children are a gift from the Lord. I never wanted to have kids. I always thought that I'd be a terrible mom. When I turned 24 and really started living for God, He began to show me that I can do all things through Him (Philippians 4:13). I had one son. Then when I was pregnant with my daughter, God asked me, "Why would you quit having children when they are going to be soldiers for me?" Uuuuuuuummmmm, because I don't want anymore! But I yielded to God and told him that I would sacrifice my body and that it would be His vessel to do with as he willed. So now I have five kids! After number three, I figured, who doesn't want a gift? I love gifts! So if children are a gift from God, what greater gift can I have? I will take all your gifts, God! Y'all! My kids are the greatest part of me. They amplify everything that is beautiful. It is hard some days. It was devastatingly hard as a widow with five kids. Sometimes, I don't want to be "mom," but I am so very grateful that I get the chance to be a part of something that is greater than me and get to invest in these super cool people. I can't wait to see what God does with, in, and through my children. I get nervous sometimes because I know my God, and sacrifice is part of His story, which is hard to accept when you have children that it may be a part of their story too. I have to trust that in all things, especially with my children and their personal journey with Him, that He is good (Psalm 107:1).

<u>Abortion</u>

Just the other day I had a conversation with my daughter about abortion, and she told me, "It's just a clump of cells." I said, "Fancy that my clump of cells is standing here telling me that it's just a clump of cells." That "clump of cells" has an intricate design and divine purpose. They are not an accident, and they are not just because you had sex. There are many people who have had sex and have not gotten pregnant. Sex is the designed avenue used by God to create inside of us, but it is by God that life is chosen to exist.

We all start somewhere. At the beginning of creation, it was void. But that doesn't mean it couldn't become something amazing and wonderful once God spoke into it. I think one of the biggest travesties of abortion is the lack of dreaming with God about the potential hidden within the clump of cells. We were all, once, a clump of cells. We were all, once, only full of potential. I am even bold enough to say without Jesus, you are still only full of potential but haven't yet reached your fullness because only by Him do you fulfill your unique divine purpose. Does that remove your value? Absolutely not! Not any more than those "clump of cells" have a reduced value because they have potential that isn't fully recognized.

You won't find the statement "do not kill your unborn babies" in the Bible. But in Exodus 21:22–25, there is a scripture that says if a pregnant woman is struck during the scuffle of two men that whatever happens to the baby should also happen to the man who caused it. So if the baby dies, the attacker must die—a life for a life. If the baby is bruised, then you bruise the man, etc. This is quite a powerful acknowledgement of the value of an unborn child for equal punishment to be carried out against a full-grown man. Of course, a full-grown man in that day was extremely valuable, so this scripture is stating that the unborn child has the same value as the most valuable man.

Which then begs the question: Is God pro-life? I don't think so, and scripture reports that He often calls for the death of people for many different reasons. So I don't think God has an issue with humans dying, as long as He is the one calling the shots. I think God's issue with abortion is that it has nothing to do with Him. Abortion is us playing God with His gifts. We already saw in the last section that children are a gift. God is very clear that He is the *only* God (Exodus 20:3, Isaiah 45:5–7, Revelation 22:13). When He makes something, it isn't up to us to question his motivation and certainly not to destroy the thing at will. My daughter is about to be 16, and I got her a car. When I gave her the keys, I said, "This is actually my car. I bought it. I pay for the insurance, and it is in my name. But I want you to enjoy it and have it as your own. But if at any point you mistreat or take advantage of the car, I will take it back from you. This is a privilege and not something that I owe you." I believe this is how God feels about giving us babies. He gives us a gift to enjoy and be a part of the journey, but if we take advantage, if we abuse or neglect the gift or if we destroy it, then we will be held accountable for that.

So we can argue all day long on when and whether there is a heartbeat and whether it is murder or all the other things that make us feel justified or in control, but really, these are just attempts at justifying playing God and not participating in His creation and dreams for this world that He created. It is an abuse of the gift. I'd err on the side of caution and just know that if God created it, He has a purpose for it and maybe we should let God be God and let Him do what He does best with His creation. He gave us dominion and power, but he did not give us His throne.

<u>Worshiping celebrities</u>

We were created to worship (Psalm 150:6). God put the desire to worship in our hearts because the worship was meant for Him. Since we worship anything that we desire, if we desire fame and glamor, and recognition, we can end up worshiping celebrities. Celebrities in our modern culture give us a fantasy to desire. They create art that makes us dream, and then they seem to have endlessly glamorous lives that we attempt to live vicariously through. They are the epitome of what we have been deceived to believe that we should all have. However, it is a lie. It is a false sense of importance. Truly, the devil has used it as a great distraction from the One who deserves our worship and praise.

God first tells us in Exodus what His expectations are regarding worship.

²I am the Lord your God, who brought you out of the land of Egypt, out of the house of slavery. ³ You shall have no other gods before me. ⁴ You shall not make for yourself a carved image, or any likeness of anything that is in heaven above, or that is in the earth beneath, or that is in the water under the earth. ⁵ You shall not bow down to them or serve them, for I the Lord your God am a jealous God, visiting the iniquity of the fathers on the children to the third and the fourth generation of those who hate me, ⁶ but showing steadfast love to thousands of those who love me and keep my commandments. (Exodus 20: 1–4 ESV)

We can get lost in idol worship when we see celebrities as more than mere humans doing a job. We don't even know the people in person, yet we can become totally consumed with who they are, what they are doing, and how they look. This momentarily fills an inner desire to connect with someone that we think is greater than us. But we were made to have that desire for God and Him alone.

Why do you think God says he is a jealous God? It seems like God wouldn't have anything to be jealous of, yet he tells us that he is jealous in the same passage that he is telling us not to worship anything or anyone else. He knew that our hearts are prone to wander toward worshiping anything that we can grasp with our minds. He wants our hearts to be solely bent toward worshiping Him because only He is worthy of that devotion and honor. So if you catch yourself wrapped up in the worship of celebrities or lost in infinite newsreels, I challenge you to turn off the TV, put down the phone, open up your Bible, and dive into meeting your God. He will not let you down.

Set boundaries around how much you expose yourself to anything that is taking you away from God and His purpose for you. You may feel like you are detoxing, just like the diversion was a drug. That is when you know that you have indeed put priorities in the wrong order, and then you can begin to put healthy priorities in the correct order, with God being first. As you set more and more boundaries to put God first and everything else second or third, you will experience more and more freedom and more and more ability to be overall healthy in mind, body, and spirit.

How to treat those who are different from us

In today's culture, the way in which many American citizens have failed to help others and care for their plight has been brought to light.

> [37] And he said to him, "You shall love the Lord your God with all your heart and with all your soul and with all your mind. [38] This is the great and first commandment. [39] And a second is like it: You shall love your neighbor as yourself. [40] On these two commandments depend all the Law and the Prophets." (Matthew 22:37–40 ESV)

The beginning of this verse also addresses the last section where a call was given to love God first, before anyone or anything else. I saved it for this section because I thought it was a good segue to tie these ideas together. Once we love God with all of us and we are devoting our worship only to Him, our perspective of our neighbor becomes much more vast. That is why, in this passage, the two ideas are connected. The greatest commandment is to love God with all your heart, mind, body, and soul. The reason is He, alone, is worthy of our praise, and He, alone, can handle being all consumed by our love without failing us. Humans will fail us every time, so when we put humans where our God shaped hole is, we set ourselves up for ultimate disappointment.

But loving our neighbor as ourselves? What does that even mean? You may think that you don't even like your neighbor. Ha! Let's look at God's heart on who our neighbor is: The account in Luke, most commonly known as the parable of the Good Samaritan, explains the heart that we should have toward our neighbor. This account is of Jesus and a lawyer talking:

29 But he, desiring to justify himself, said to Jesus, "And who is my neighbor?" 30 Jesus replied, "A man was going down from Jerusalem to Jericho, and he fell among robbers, who stripped him and beat him and departed, leaving him half dead. 31 Now by chance a priest was going down that road, and when he saw him he passed by on the other side. 32 So likewise a Levite, when he came to the place and saw him, passed by on the other side. 33 But a Samaritan, as he journeyed, came to where he was, and when he saw him, he had compassion. [34] He went to him and bound up his wounds, pouring on oil and wine. Then he set him on his own animal and brought him to an inn and took care of him. [35] And the next day he took out two denarii and gave them to the innkeeper, saying, 'Take care of him, and whatever more you spend, I will repay you when I come back.' [36] Which of these three, do you think, proved to be a neighbor to the man who fell among the robbers?" [37] He said, "The one who showed him mercy." And Jesus said to him, "You go, and do likewise." (Luke 10:25–37 ESV)

The man in this parable is unidentified by race, religion, or any other defining factor, so we don't know who the beaten man is, and Jesus specifically left out any defining characteristics because the man could be any of us. Then Jesus specifies a priest as the first to walk past. This man represents a man of God that should know to love on this man, but he can't be bothered. Maybe he had somewhere more important to be. Maybe he didn't want to get his ceremonial robes dirty. Maybe he had an appointment to pray over someone. We don't know anything more than he just couldn't be bothered, and he made sure to pass the man on the other side of the road. How many times have you passed someone on the proverbial other side of the road so as not to be bothered by their plight? I think this is probably the closest to Christians today who give to non-profits—to support those who actually are doing the work in the trenches—rather than traveling to those places where the needs are vast. Giving to non-profits is a great work and definitely needed;

however, are we just passing by on the "other side of the street" and not willing to get our hands dirty if necessary. Please know that I am not trying to discourage you from giving to non-profits but more trying to encourage you to jump in and help!

Next to pass is the Levite. The Levites are descendants of Levi and hold a special, set apart, place in the Jewish religious community. The Levites are not as high as the priest, yet they are important people in the community. This Levite also passed on the other side of the road, so as not to be bothered, but maybe it was more for his own image. Maybe this Levite was scared someone would misunderstand the situation. Maybe this Levite just didn't really know how to help, so he ignored that there was a need for help. Maybe he decided he would pray for the man. Maybe he thought he would get help for him in the next place. I don't know. Scripture doesn't expound on what was happening with the Levite man, but I think this also happens frequently in the modern Christian community. "I'll pray for you" becomes a passive way of not helping. It removes the guilt of the one praying, but it does absolutely nothing physically for the one lying there wounded. Again, prayer is a wonderful and powerful part of our participation relationship with God, but sometimes, we need to get our hands dirty and physically get in the game with people that are hurting and in need. We often look for others to be the ones helping, a common theme among American Christians because we just don't want to be bothered. We are just too busy. We want someone else to do the hard work with our good intentions.

Now we come to the Samaritan. Jesus points out that it was a Samaritan because they were "those people," the ones no Jew would interact with back in Jesus' day. They held no important status, and they were not well respected by Jewish people. Yet, he is the one to have compassion on this man. His day might have been full to the brim with responsibility, yet he paused. He stopped. He helped. He rescued the fellow image-bearer. He didn't ask if the man was worthy of help; he just did literally everything it took to make him better. He went as far as paying the inn person wages and then promised to cover whatever else would be owed for him. This man loved his neighbor with compassion. We love our neighbor the same way when we are actively generous with our time, money, means, and ourselves.

Loving our neighbor isn't just about the person who lives next door, though they are included. Loving your neighbor is looking past yourself to the needs of others in your neighborhood, city, state, country and globally.

We will encounter people we don't like, but it is still our job to love them. So how do we do that? This is a hard question. I think this is one of the hardest things we are called to do as a Christian.

> *⁴⁴ But I tell you, love your enemies and pray for those who persecute you, ⁴⁵ that you may be children of your Father in heaven. He causes his sun to rise on the evil and the good, and sends rain on the righteous and the unrighteous. ⁴⁶ If you love those who love you, what reward will you get? Are not even the tax collectors doing that? ⁴⁷ And if you greet only your own people, what are you doing more than others? Do not even pagans do that? (Matthew 5:44–47 NIV)*

We execute ourselves, acting as judge and jury, when we refuse to love our enemies. Let God be God. Let Him decide who should get what and how. Just as this scripture states, you aren't doing anything miraculous if you just love the people who love you. That is easy. But to love someone whom you do not like, or who is an enemy, that is entirely different and takes a power much greater than ourselves.

We can have healthy boundaries here and still honor God. If there is a harmful situation, you can actively pray for the person without being involved with them. As a matter of fact, I would suggest prayer is the place you start anytime you don't like someone. Pray for your heart and for theirs. Prayer is one of the most powerful tools that we have, and when we wield it consistently, it moves things in the spirit realm. Loving your enemy won't come from the power of yourself. It will take the Spirit intervening for you. It will come with a new place of humility, and you may even find that your heart is softened toward them after a period of time in prayer. Try it! Prayer may be the best boundary put into place for a relationship with an enemy.

Cancel culture

I am not a big fan of the "cancel culture." I find it to be rather wimpy actually. It is a way of discrediting others' experiences or opinions. Boundaries are good and helpful and don't require you to "cancel" anyone. Boundaries may require you to have space or even to end a relationship, not based on their thinking or beliefs but based on what is safe for you. While cancel culture says that if someone or something is "toxic" to our "modern" sensibilities, you just write them off and even tear them down or bash them in the process. The trouble, of course, is that there is no benchmark by which to determine what is "toxic" and what is not, and so people are attempting to erase valid historical items, parks, and people from our collective consciousness. Whether we agree with the cultural living of the past eras or not, to learn from them is important. In contrast to the whimsy of "cancel culture," boundaries require that you remain in a peaceful place within your space, that you shouldn't interact with a toxic person in any way, or maybe only from a safe distance. "Canceling" someone removes their humanity and yours. All of us have had moments that we are ashamed of, and if you haven't , just live a little longer, it will happen. This modern cultural concept has corrupted grace and forgiveness.

Politics

Politics. Oh! This is a hot topic these days. As of this writing, President Trump has just left office and President Biden is beginning the presidential office. Needless to say, this time is a hot bed for politics and the division that it can cause. Cancel culture will cause you to turn your back on your family, friends, and anyone who doesn't agree with your stance. We hear key phrases like "If you're silent, you agree," "You're phobic if you disagree," "My body, my right," and "You are responsible for my health."

This is a cancel-culture mentality and all of these are stinkin' thinkin'. They have a gaslighting undertone.

Gaslighting is the act of altering reality and then trying to make someone else confused about the situation. The actual definition according to Dictionary.com is "to cause a person to doubt his/her sanity through the use of psychological manipulation." The term comes from a movie from 1944 called *Gaslight*. In the movie, the husband alters the gaslights in the house, brightening and dimming them and then tells his wife that she is imagining the flickering. Gaslighting has become a more commonly used term as more and more of our communication lacks genuine truth and is based on emotional manipulation.

So how do these statements have a gaslighting undertone? Because these statements aren't true and are used to emotionally manipulate.

Choosing Silence

If someone is silent, that can mean many things, but one can't assume what their silence means. Often people accuse others of being silent because they have projected onto them their own thinking and perspective. The accused were silent. They said nothing; it was only the outward voice projecting onto them an assumption but not a fact.

But really maybe someone stayed silent because they don't feel safe sharing their reasons, but that doesn't mean they haven't talked to others about their feelings or emotions. They don't owe anyone, and certainly, they don't owe social media, a response.

Maybe they aren't passionate about the situation at all. Maybe they are just curious to listen to others and gather information. Silence is sometimes the wise thing. The Bible says to be quick to listen and slow to speak (James 1:19). Silence is an element of wisdom, but the world won't recognize it as such because it counters what they want to hear. Silence is their boundary and no one is able to dictate for us what is an acceptable boundary.

People are allowed to disagree with others, but that doesn't make them afraid of the situation or person or lifestyle. Earlier I told you that Jesus said we will be hated because of our call to disagree with others who are worldly. Interestingly, my brother and I had a conversation about this subject. It kind of sets a fire in me. We got out a Merriam Webster's Collegiate Dictionary, 10th edition, from 1993, and if you look up "phobic" it says, "1. Exaggerated fear of something (acrophobia), 2. Intolerance or aversion for (photophobia)." That's it. But if you look at Dictionary.com's definition of phobic in 2021, it'll say "to have a dislike or disrespect for a thing, idea, person, or group." Hmmm. I don't think the word "phobic" has actually changed in meaning that much, but it is now used to discredit another's perspective. Phobias have always meant to have a fear of something. But how did disagreeing and being afraid become synonymous? I can have a phobia of spiders, and I'm merely afraid of them; I certainly don't disagree with them. Accusing someone who disagrees of actually being afraid removes the ability of that person to have a genuine thought based on experience or faith and says that the person is operating solely out of fear, the logic being that if the fear were removed, then the person would agree. This is gaslighting in its most heinous form.

"My Body, My Right" stance

The "My body, my right" stance is a manipulation of the freedom of our bodies. We have free will, and with that, we can indeed make choices for ourselves. However, we can't use that term as a way to not accept responsibility for our actions, choices, and behaviors. This phrase tends to diminish the impact that our choices have on us and those around us. At a certain level, your body does belong to you, but if you are married, your body doesn't solely belong to you anymore (1 Corinthians 7:4). You gave your body to another to be one, and that person has a say (there is safe space for boundaries here too). Likewise, a pregnant woman now shares her body with the little person growing inside her. They are two different people sharing the same space.

Rights often stop for one where the rights for another start. Babies are completely independent of their mother's body. Believe me! I know! I have five children. Being dependent on another doesn't remove their humanity. If it did, you could say that an elderly person or a handicapped person who needs complete care is then not valid as a person. Refusing to acknowledge the blow of what abortion is doesn't change that it is indeed murder of a person. I am pro-woman and pro-life. I believe in full redemption for women who have had abortions. If you have had an abortion, I want you to know that your Father loves you so much. Your Father God will grieve with you and love you through it and through Jesus you have full forgiveness. We talked about how forgiveness calls for repentance, so if you have had an abortion, please pray the following with me:

Lord,
I recognize and acknowledge your full sovereignty and I took liberty
with the freedoms you have given me. I broke an image-bearer Lord
and I am so sorry. I repent from the depths of my heart for my actions.
The brokenness within me propelled me in ignorance to do what I
thought was best at the time, but Lord, knowing you, my heart knows
that I was wrong. I will honor you from this day on with the gifts that
you give me. Even in fear, I will walk in trust, Lord.
In Jesus' name
Amen

"It's not for me but for you" stance

This new idea, since the pandemic started, that someone else is responsible for your health might be the most laughable, most codependent and the most obnoxious new key phrase. This is sparked out of our desperate need for control. If we are responsible for someone else's health, then it is our fault if they live or die. However, we don't have the power to give life or death to anyone. That is solely according to the discretion of God. This is not referring to murder, so please don't get sidetracked. I am talking about basic control of someone else's life, so release yourself from that responsibility. As believers, if we trust that God set our days before we ever took a breath, then can you trust that when someone dies, that God already had that planned out? You know what you can do? Do you know what you do have control over? Your faith. Pray for them to get up from the dead. We have that authority. (Matthew 10:8) People are going to die. We are spiritual beings here on Earth for a season of time but this isn't our home or destination. The reason this phrase "it's not for me but to keep you safe" has become so popular is to make others feel guilty or control by proxy.

We need to be able to have a long-term focus and not allow others to manipulate our emotions or feelings about control we don't genuinely have.

Implementing boundaries

Much of the discussion surrounding these topics in our culture is embedded with gaslighting, saying that if you do a certain action or behavior, it is because you care about others, and if you do not do the action or behavior, it is because you do not care about others. Caring for others is a vast and broad spectrum term that can look like a huge array of things. To judge someone quickly is quite a foolish thing to do because you truly don't know motives without asking.

All of these statements are based on judgmental thinking and projection. Projection is when you tell someone else who they are and what they think, not based on their own merit or thought, but on yours. This is not healthy boundary thinking. Healthy boundary thinking is to take someone at their face value, and then decide how you can be involved in that relationship in a healthy way. Let's look at the contrast.

Healthy boundaries do not require emotions even on hot topics. If someone has a completely different opinion than you on, say, politics, you then assess at what level you can discuss politics with this person. No need to judge or critique their thinking. If someone mildly disagrees with you and you are able to talk with that person without getting into a fight, then you may be able to have some interesting conversation that both of you may learn from. However, if someone mildly disagrees with you and every time you try to talk, you end up fighting with each other, you need to set a boundary: I cannot talk politics with you because you and I cannot get along and cannot treat each other with respect. I will not talk politics with you any longer. There is no projection, gaslighting, name-calling, or judging necessary. If the person was to try to engage you again in a political conversation, you can remove yourself from the party, dinner, or whatever social setting you may find yourself in.

> Setting boundaries is hard at first. It may seem like you are wimping out. But over time, you begin to have so much more control over your emotions and yourself and will find that, what was once so unpleasant to participate in, isn't bad after all. You begin to realize you have control! Control where it rightfully resides: over yourself. One fruit of the spirit is self-control (Galatians 5:22–23).

If you interact with someone who highly disagrees with you and you feel attacked every time that person is around, you will need a stronger boundary. You would verbally tell the person, "I feel attacked when we spend time together, so for now, I think it's best that we don't spend time around each other." This kind of situation is harder because it requires genuine conversation and even slight confrontation. If you don't feel like you can talk to the person that you feel attacked by, maybe having someone help you state your boundary is helpful. Your spouse could help you or one of your children or a parent. These relationships are often close enough that they can help without creating further drama. If none of this support exists for you, then you may have to just remove yourself from the relationship. Giving the other person the chance to realize that you feel attacked is a good way to start, but some people can't be reasoned with.

Projection, gaslighting, name-calling, and judging do not have to be a part of your boundary-making. The point of boundaries isn't to be mean or unkind but to create safety for your heart, soul, mind, and body. Proverbs 4:23 tells us to protect our hearts because all of life comes out of our hearts. Boundaries are how we establish that protection.

It is not only OK but absolutely critical to put boundaries around cultural corruptions. Sin is only going to get worse and abound in our world. We must be able to stand firm. One of my personal boundaries that I have chosen since all these topics have become so much in the forefront is, honor God first, man second (Matthew 6:33). I don't have to walk around bashing anyone or any lifestyle, but I also don't have to celebrate, encourage, or acknowledge it if it goes against God's standards and principles. It isn't being mean or unkind or judgmental; it is a boundary of honoring my Father first. Remember, Jesus tells us that we will be hated because of our beliefs just as He was. It's OK. You will have less confusion when you set your standards based on God's standards.

God is the ultimate authority, and He sets the standard. Just like the laws of our land set a standard by which we are to obey. I never feel the need to apologize if someone gets a ticket when the sign says 50 mph, and they are going 75 mph. I didn't make the speed limit, I didn't set the authority in place, but if I am a representative of that authority (meaning I'm a cop), I am just supposed to uphold it. As God's representative, it is my role to uphold it. As the world turns more and more away from His standards, it will cause more and more clashing with the people who are holding the line for God. These people are also called missionaries. We are on a mission to share God and Jesus and him crucified and resurrected with everyone, and to do that, we uphold God's boundaries, which will cause us to look and sound and act differently than the world in many ways.

Actionable Items:

- What are three areas that you struggle with culture and your belief system?
- Study what scripture says about these areas. Write it down.
- Write three proclamations down for your boundaries in these areas.

Visit my website for examples and more!

Chapter 10

Relationship Boundaries Matter

<u>Defining the relationship</u>

Sometimes people have roles in our lives for a season. It is OK when the season has completed to let them go. You may not rename them into another relationship like Jesus did, but you can know that it is OK to let them go.

In John 19:25–27, Jesus is on the cross. He looks at his mom and tells her that the disciple standing with her is now her son, and then he tells the disciple that she is now his mother. Jesus is redefining the relationship between these two people. His purpose and mission was primarily to be the Savior of the world, so when He was about to complete his mission, He created the boundary that He was no longer the son of Mary but the Son of God, and Savior for us all. He didn't want to leave His mom without a son, and He didn't want to leave his disciple without purpose. Releasing himself and giving them to each other created a boundary that He was now separate from them and that they didn't lose relational standing but gained each other.

How might this be applicable in your life? I had some friends growing up. I thought of them like sisters. They were my go-to people, much like Mary and John would have been for Jesus. We hung out together all the time, but I wouldn't say the relationship was always healthy. In fact, looking back on it, it was generally not healthy at all. I knew nothing about boundaries growing up. I always thought that my advice was well needed. I mean, who doesn't want brilliant advice regularly?? My friends. That's who. I just wanted to help them out. I just wanted to make things better for them, but I wasn't. I was just wasting my breath and frustrating myself and probably irritating the fire out of them. I had no concept of boundaries at the time. As I got older and began to understand boundaries a bit more, I would sometimes leave a conversation with one of them thinking, "Why am I even friends with her?" As time went on, I realized that I didn't have to be friends with her anymore. It wasn't that I didn't care about her or that I no longer loved her, we just were not a good fit relationally. I found myself frustrated with her more often than at peace, and I am sure she was tired of my relentless advice, which she never listened to anyway. I knew that I could walk away and the girls would have each other to fall back on, and it was relieving for me. I was able to free myself and them.

Sometimes, you may need to free others from you. If you catch yourself being the advice-giver on a regular basis and find yourself frustrated that no one is listening to you, you may need to free them from yourself. This is a healthy boundary for you. This boundary doesn't require you to cut anyone off necessarily, but just to realize that it isn't your issue anymore and that you don't have to be the problem-solver for others unsolicited. You can ask if someone would like your advice, and if they say, "Why are you asking me that?! You always give it to me anyway!" This is a great time to share your new boundary. You might say, "I know I have always given unsolicited advice. I realize that it might be unwelcome, so from now on before I give any advice, I am going to ask if you actually want it." This will potentially open a conversation that may be super beneficial for everyone. Our boundaries can be a good influence on others when they see that boundaries aren't meant for harm but for good.

There are many other situations in which you may need to redefine the relationship and create a boundary with your friends. You may need to move your best friend to a casual friend or casual friend to a social media friend; or you may need to remove them from your friend list entirely.

You may be in a situation where the friend is also family, like a sister-in-law. I know two ladies who are friends and sisters-in-law. I know they love each other, but because their personalities don't necessarily complement each other, they have to be careful with their relationship. When the sister-in-law visits from out of town, the hostess often puts aside her own preferences and opinions to make the sister-in-law have a good visit and experience. These are sacrificial boundaries. The hostess is choosing to put herself aside, not in a doormat or unsafe way, to make sure that her relationship can remain calm and peaceful.

My mentor and dear friend has a situation with a grieving friend that has challenged her friendship boundaries. When she invited the grieving friend to a family function, the friend cornered one of my mentor's grown children and proceeded to dump a lot of emotional garbage onto her son. The son couldn't figure out how to get away from the lady and visit with his siblings that he doesn't get to see often. My mentor was able to see the desperation in her son's eyes and rescued him. However, there was a very sour taste left from that situation and now she has an internal struggle over whether she can invite her friend to any more family functions.

I told my dear friend that she should set her boundaries with the lady by telling her that when their family gets together, it is for celebration and that heavy emotional stuff is best left for other times. My friend told me that she wasn't necessarily comfortable doing that because she felt she would hurt her feelings. So I gave my friend a visual image to help her understand how boundaries would be beneficial. I told her that her family is on a ship (the gathering) and the grieving lady is in the ocean (being left out of the gathering). If she gives the lady some boundaries, she has thrown a lifeline to the lady and given her the opportunity to take it. The lady in the metaphorical ocean can take the lifeline and join in on the gatherings if she can respect that they are meant to be celebratory, or she can choose to stay alone. However, if no lifeline is offered, that may not be entirely fair to the lady because she may be left wondering why she is no longer invited to future gatherings, never realizing how her emotional baggage dump affected the family.

Boundaries are not always about keeping things out, but sometimes they are the lifeline that you can offer someone struggling. Keeping safety lines around yourself and others is the goal, but you don't have to lock someone out entirely to make your point. You can give a lifeline offer with understood boundaries and give that person the chance to decide if it works well for them. If not, you still hold your line and move on.

Career-based relationships

Some of our outward relationships we choose, like our friends, and some we get by default when we choose a job. These relationships can be fun and rewarding or complicated and rocky. Boundaries applied in these relationships can make the relationships thrive. The good news is that the lines are not as often blurred when we are dealing with outward relationships. We can quit a job or transfer departments if we need to get away from an unhealthy relationship. We can quit talking to friends if we need to gain peace and perspective if things are going sideways in that relationship.

Clearly defining your boundaries with bosses, coworkers, and employees is a good tactic to help the relationship thrive. For example, if your boss is putting more work on you than you can handle, let them know with a clearly stated email what you are able to accomplish in your job. A boss that wants to see you succeed will help you achieve. A boss that is trying to overstep and pressure you too much is probably not suited for you. Now, don't confuse a boss trying to push you out of your comfort zone a little to stretch you and teach you as being the same as a boss who just doesn't care about your boundaries. Bosses usually are in the position to challenge their staff, and a good one should push you to grow but not push you to the brink of breaking.

If coworkers are creating a negative environment and workspace, remove yourself as quickly as possible. When someone is talking negatively in a work environment, they usually have an ulterior motive. It may be to sabotage the boss or make others feel insignificant or not valued in the company. Boundaries will keep you safe and keep your job safe when the other coworkers know that you will not engage in unhealthy and negative conversations. This may be one of the most freeing aspects of any workplace environment. You have the ability to choose what you participate in!

It is important not to gossip in the workplace. A coworker will not have power over you if you refuse to engage in banter or gossip. Additionally, we do not bring honor to ourselves or others when we gossip about others. Many scriptures in the Bible talk about refraining from gossip (2 Corinthians 12:20, Ephesians 4:29, James 1:26, James 4:11). Use these scriptures as reminders: make notes and stick them on your desk if you need to. Protecting yourself and others from gossip applies to all relationships, family, friends, and coworkers alike.

If you are the boss, you need to set boundaries with your employees. Employees usually look to the leader to set the environment of the workplace. Outside of having an employee that is hell-bent on making the environment toxic, the boss or leader will create the direction that others align behind. Employees need to have a structure built into their job descriptions so they know where the lines are drawn. Sometimes, as companies change and possibly grow, your employees may not grow with you. It is OK to let that employee move to another job. Setting the boundaries to keep employees in alignment with the growth of a business or culture that a business is trying to establish is of the utmost importance for the company. If there is an allowance for an employee to poison the workplace, the entire company will pay a price for it. Be it losing good employees, closing, or not producing to capacity, there is always a price for allowing an employee to cross boundaries.

Jesus often had to remind the disciples of his purpose for coming here. In Matthew 16:23 Jesus said to Peter, "Get behind me, Satan," when Peter was questioning Jesus' purpose and goal. Those are quite harsh words for someone who has dedicated their life to following Him. Why would Jesus be so harsh? Maybe Jesus wasn't harsh. Maybe Jesus was defining a strong line, giving Peter a boundary so Peter never again misunderstood that there is an order and structure to the purpose that they were all living out. If you are the boss, I probably wouldn't suggest you use this exact phrase to an employee, but maybe finding what fits the company's purpose, culture, and goal and setting the hard line in the proverbial sand is appropriate.

Never underestimate the power that boundaries can have in the workplace with the people who you may spend more time with than your own family. Every relationship you have needs boundaries. Use the boundaries to keep the relationships safe and healthy.

Importance of family boundaries

Family is such a complicated subject matter for most people. We don't pick our family—God does that—and we are expected to honor our family. But that doesn't mean your family has the freedom to violate you in any way. Remember, freedom doesn't mean a free-for-all. Yes, we have freedom as Jesus came to set us free (Galatians 5:1). We are free in Christ, and we have the freedom to protect our hearts in any way we need to. Protecting ourselves is not the same as hurting someone else. When we protect ourselves, the goal is not to deliberately be mean or hateful or harmful to another person. Self-protection can be a fine balance between healthily setting boundaries and hurting others with an impenetrable guard around us. Boundaries help to establish where the lines are that cannot be crossed within relationships. Boundaries are not to create a forcefield around us so that we cannot have a relationship with anyone. Boundaries are for us, not to control others. This applies to parenting, marriage, and even to your children.

When I was praying about this section, God just kept taking me to Tamar. There are two stories in the Bible about women named Tamar. One is a princess, and one is not. Neither of them is flattering, and both are super intense. I love the Old Testament because it shows how God can use the hottest of messes for his purposes. It also shows that none of us is perfect and that He doesn't need us to be perfect; He just needs us to be willing. The culture of the Old Testament is vastly different than ours today, so I am not using these stories to necessarily show how boundaries were used but more how boundaries were not used.

Our first encounter with Tamar is in Genesis 38. Please feel free to go read the whole story, but I am going to give you the summarized version. Judah and Shua have three sons, Er, the first born, Onan, and Shelah. Judah picked out a wife for Er named Tamar. Er was evil in the sight of God. It doesn't specify how, but God took Er's life prematurely. Judah then told Onan to go and take Tamar, as was the custom of a Levirate marriage. The brother-in-law would take on the widow so the firstborn would have an heir of the same blood line. Onan wasn't exactly happy about this arrangement and wasn't very fond of his evil older brother, Er. He decided that he would "let his seed fall to the ground" and not allow Tamar to get pregnant by him. This was a big no-no in the eyes of God, so God took Onan's life too.

Well, needless to say, Judah was scared to death to give Tamar his youngest son, Shelah. Judah told Tamar to wait at her father's house until Shelah was grown, and then he would give her to Shelah. However, Judah did not honor his word. During this delay, he became a widower as well. Tamar was informed that Judah was going to Timnah to shear his sheep, and she got crafty. She dressed as a harlot and met up with Judah. Judah asked if he could lie with her, and she made him promise that he would pay her. She asked him for his seal, cord, and staff. All of these items would have been specific to Judah. His seal was most likely his ring; the cord would have been colored to represent his family; and his staff was what he used to shepherd his flock, which he was leading there to be sheared. It would have had an emblem on it, much like farmers today have a mark for their cattle and flocks.

He slept with her, and she conceived twins. About three months later, Judah heard that she was pregnant, and he was furious. He commanded that she be brought to him and be killed. She sent the items to Judah and informed him that she was pregnant by the man who owned these items. Judah saw his folly in not giving her to his son, Shelah, for because of this Tamar felt she had no other option than deception in order to have Judah do right by her.

Wow! What a hot mess we have here. We have a father with two dead sons and a widow desperate not to be pushed to the side. How many times do our families face these same kinds of fears? It might not be the same dramatic events, but we have a father afraid of not stepping up, a daughter that is manipulating to not get left behind, and brothers having competition and resentments toward each other. Really you could put any sibling group in there, and it might be fitting for your family. If Judah had done what he said he would do, maybe the situation would've been fine and we would've never had this story in the Bible. Shelah and Tamar might've gone on to have three sons as well and an heir for the family, and life would've just moved forward. That would have been the easy story, but because we are humans, we don't often follow the easy story.

Judah tried to manipulate as well by not sending for Tamar when Shelah was grown. He blamed Tamar for the deaths of his sons instead of seeing that they had both done evil in the sight of God. His blame shifted onto Tamar. She was an easy target. She was a woman, and in her relationship with his two sons, they had ended up dead. However, Tamar didn't kill them. She did nothing wrong at all. She was merely the recipient of a crappy set of circumstances. Why was she the one to blame? I think we often need to blame someone so badly for bad or sad things that we will blame anyone close to us, or we will blame anyone that is merely available to be blamed in the situation. Judah placing blame on Tamar was one of his biggest mistakes and it changed the trajectory of the rest of his life. Have you blamed someone in your family to account for a wrong in your life? Is it time to release them? If so, pray with me:

Lord,
I blame_____ for_____, and
I can't let it go. I will only be able to let it go by your mercy and
grace. I will release them for the sake of myself and my heart. I
trust that you know all truth and that I do not have to keep or hold
others accountable for things I cannot control. I am going to rest in
you and offer freedom and full forgiveness to_____.
Blame is a painful weight to carry even though my pride feeds off

of it. I will release myself from having to rectify a situation that was devastating.
In Jesus' name,
Amen

Blame is a stronghold for our pride. It doesn't serve any other purpose than to put the difficult situation onto another person. Maybe it is actually their fault, but unfortunately, they will never account to you. You must let God be God and know that nothing gets past Him. Our pride will keep us shackled to the blame game. It will weigh your heart down. Pray this prayer over and over and over again until you have been able to truly let it go. Forgiveness always has a call to repentance, but even if the person you blame doesn't repent, you can still forgive. Sometimes situations are so horrific that it seems impossible to forgive. The power of the Holy Spirit can work in you in ways that you cannot work in yourself. Give it all to God.

If Judah had released himself from the blame game, he would have freed up Tamar and given her to his next son. He would have been honorable. But instead blame and fear kept him locked up, and truly, it made him vulnerable to her manipulation. She had become desperate. Desperation leads people to do things that are not necessarily in keeping with their character. She wanted her way. She found a way to make that happen. It was through her manipulation that Judah became aware of his own sin against her.

Tamar was a widow stuck at her dad's house. She wasn't wanted there, most likely because she couldn't be married off again. Plus she no longer belonged to her father's house, but to Judah's house. So, she probably didn't feel very wanted. These are just suppositions based on the culture at the time. She had had a promise made to her, but it didn't seem like it was going to be kept. She had already lost two husbands, which had taken a toll on her heart and mind. She was like a tumbleweed just blowing in the wind but going nowhere. So she plotted.

She ended up manipulating, taking on a false identity to trick Judah. She was wise in her trickery. She knew that the items would come in handy and that they would spare her life. Why didn't she reveal herself that night? Because she first needed to ensure she was pregnant. An heir was what she needed. If she had not become pregnant, she would not have had the same power play. She was putting all her eggs in one basket, pun intended. It was her way back to freedom. It was her way back to where she belonged. Oh how she must've longed to have freedom again! It was worth the gamble to earn her freedom again. When Judah's pride settled on the blame game, she felt she had no other option than to manipulate. How many times have you felt like manipulation was your last and best option? Maybe your only option? It isn't. Manipulation can be so hurtful. We don't get the rest of the story of how their relationship played out, but if she continued to manipulate to get her way, it is doubtful that their marriage was a happy one.

In all of God's beauty, He always has a redemption plan in place. God gave Judah two more sons through Tamar. God redeemed his losses through the woman he blamed. Notice I said "redeemed," not "replaced." People we love can't be replaced, but the heart can be redeemed. God also gave Tamar the heir that she so desperately needed to gain her freedom and place in the family. God did not honor their wrong choices, but through His grace, He redeemed His beloved children. One of Tamar's twin children, Perez, is in the lineage of Jesus.

Family can seem to change the game when it comes to boundaries, but holding your boundaries is still critical. This story has all sorts of boundary crossing and that led to some craziness in their lives. However, this story seems somewhat mild compared to the Tamar we meet next.

In 2 Samuel 13, we meet our second Tamar, who is the protagonist in one of the greatest tragedies in the Bible. God wants me to share this story because so many women, especially in our modern world, have a sexual assault story that needs to be heard and these women desperately need to be healed. Whether your violation is by family or someone else, daughter, you are loved and seen. God knows. Not a single second of your violation has missed his loving eyes, and He will vindicate and justify you in his perfection. Rest in that, sister. Your recourse is to find wholeness in Christ through forgiveness and establishing boundaries. Leave the rest to God.

Tamar is a beautiful woman and a princess. She is the daughter of King David. Her brother, a prince, Amnon, and his cousin, Jonadab, plot against her. At the beginning of the chapter, it mentions that Amnon physically craves his sister so much that he is sick over it. Just my thought, but that sounds like some demonic craving to me. Meanwhile, Jonadab tells Amnon to pretend to be sick and asks the king to send Tamar to attend to him and make him cakes in his presence. So the king does as his son asks and sends Tamar to attend to him. While she is there, he asks her to bring him his food into the bedroom where he is lying down. When she goes to him, he grabs a hold of her. She begs him not to take her virginity. She begs him to do right by her and not to do this disgraceful thing, for she will not be able to get rid of the reproach. Amnon, of course, doesn't care and takes what he wants: he rapes his sister. Once he is done, he discards her like trash. He kicks her out of the room and then locks the door behind her. She tears her clothes, puts ashes on her head (ash was a sign of grief in those days), and weeps loudly as she goes away.

Absalom, also a son of King David and Tamar's brother, asked if Amnon had violated her. Upon learning the truth, he became furious with his brother. Tamar took refuge in Absalom's house. Two years later, Absalom plotted a plan to kill Amnon. He asked the king to let all the sons go with him for the sheep shearing. While they were on the trip, Absalom's men killed Amnon to avenge Tamar's rape.

The Old Testament is full of people that experience things just like you and I have. Maybe your story isn't just like either of these, but if we are honest, it probably has some skeletons in the closet. Clearly, there were no healthy boundaries in this family dynamic and that led to all sorts of pain and heartache.

Amnon had no right to his sister, no matter his feelings. He didn't practice self-control, and he certainly didn't show any care or concern for her feelings, needs, or wants. Amnon violated the biggest boundary of all, which is our physical body and how it is used, touched, and handled. He forced himself upon his sister in the cruelest of ways.

If someone has done this to you, you are not responsible for it. You are not responsible for the ultimate violation of your boundary, but you will have to find the place to let it go and reestablish your boundaries for safety again. So many times, young girls and women will let the boundary be violated over and over again because the person who initially violated the boundary seemed to completely shatter and destroy it. The young ladies then feel as though the lack of boundary is so open that they can't protect themselves again.

Stay with me. Once a girl is violated as a child or young lady, there is a brokenness that happens on the inside. We see this same reaction with Tamar. She weeps loudly, tears her clothes, and puts ashes on her head. These are all signs of great distress and grief. In our culture today, we mostly expect girls to sit down and be quiet because we do not want to face the horribleness of the situation. So many women that are violated as young girls will give themself away to try to fill the gaping hole in the boundary line that has been opened. They do not have the tools to know that they can close that boundary line again, seal it tightly, and protect it, even with the gaping hole they feel is there. If you know of a young girl who is struggling, once you have learned how to put healthy boundaries in place, encourage her to establish boundaries for herself. You cannot fix her for her, as that is codependency, but you can share your journey and help her realize that she can have healthy boundaries again.

In Tamar's story, she begs her brother to ask for her the right way so she doesn't get the reproach that will surely come if she is violated. She is trying to set a boundary for her safety, but her brother will have nothing to do with it. She instead takes refuge at her other brother's house so as to not be shamed. She protected herself the best she was able. She couldn't control everything, but what she could control, she did. She is truly the hero of this story and I have great respect for her. We don't get to know the completed story of Tamar, but I hope that she had a full restoration. Clearly, if you are being violated by a family member or a friend, you need to get help immediately. Let someone safe know immediately! If you have been violated by anyone in your life sexually, will you please pray with me?

Lord,

I didn't have control over what happened to me. I was violated by the sin of someone else. They crossed the most important boundary in my life, which is my body and how it is used, touched, and handled. I am in the space now that I want to work through forgiveness and allow you to heal all the dark spaces. I recognize that I am now in control of my safety, and I do not have to wear the guilt and shame of that person. Please forgive me for any ignorance I might have had in the years after my brokenness started. I want my body to honor you first. 1 Corinthians 6:20 says that since I was bought with a price, I am to honor you with all of me. I am ready to do that with your help. I release any control I may be trying to have over a situation out of my control. Work in me, O God.

In Jesus' name,

Amen

Then we come to the hate that festers in Absalom. 1 John 3:15 says that if we have hate in our hearts, we have commited murder, which is a repeated lesson of what Jesus tells us in Matthew 5:21–22. Essentially, Absalom had murdered his brother before he did it in person. Actual physical murder is just the physical manifestation of the spiritual condition of hatred. Absalom couldn't fix what had happened to his sister. He let it fester in his heart until he committed his own heinous act, which felt much like retribution. He wanted to control something he couldn't control, so he let it turn his heart dark and ugly. This also happens to us when we want to control something in our family dynamic that we have no control over. When we can't vindicate what we think is a wrong or horrible act and we let it stew in our hearts until we hate another image-bearer, we have lost the idea of what the cross was for and who God is. Romans 12:19 is a hard pill to swallow for those of us stuck on vengeance. It says to never take your own revenge but leave room for the wrath of God; that vengeance is his and he will repay. You must let God be God. You must let go of vengeful and hateful thoughts toward someone who has done something awful. Why? Because God tells you to do so. I know that may seem like such a blanket answer and you may be thinking, "But you have no idea what I have been through!" You are right. I don't. But God does and he still tells us to let him take vengeance for us. Why should we trust God's vengeance? Because it is perfect! God can do things to people that we can't. He can get to the heart of others. He can penetrate the deepest darkest places of their hearts. Most importantly, we shouldn't desire that someone be destroyed. God will take care of it. No one will stand in front of God cocky and arrogant of themselves. It's like children standing in front of their parent when they know they have done something wrong. So just rest in the fact that our holy and just Father will be able to do exceedingly far more than what we could ever dream of in his perfect love for anyone who has hurt or harmed you. It won't look like you want it to because God is God, and he is not limited by our human confines, but I can guarantee you it will be thorough and perfect.

Absalom had options. He chose to make his life more complicated. He could have just loved on Tamar and realized that he couldn't fix what had happened. This would've been the healthiest response. He could have protected her as much as possible in the future without having anything to do with their brother. He had options. In the same way that Amnon allowed lust to gather in his heart until it became a devastating act, Absalom let hate gather in his heart until he committed a similarly heinous act.

We must choose to let the Holy Spirit keep things in the correct order, letting God be God, and hold our boundaries so that God can do the work in each person as He sees fit. Our wrath and vengeance will never satisfy our spirit and may only temporarily satisfy our flesh. This is the lesson Job helps to teach us. He had to allow God to be God. Job had to trust what he couldn't see and know that God would take care of the wrongs and redeem him.

The first Tamar story that we read was all about blame and manipulation. Maybe you recognize this pattern in your own family and the destruction that it has created. The second Tamar, our princess, was completely violated and discarded and her brother became full of hate. This tragic story may mirror some of your life experiences with your family. It can be hard to set boundaries with family when there is dysfunction, but I promise you that it will be worth the effort, no matter how difficult.

Hopefully walking through these two stories helped enlighten some areas that you may need to work on. But we aren't done with family yet! Family is always the most complicated place for boundaries because of the interconnection we have with our family.

Jesus' example of family boundaries

Jesus always managed to have good boundaries. We see this in action with his mom. In John 2, Jesus is at a wedding with his mom and disciples. When the wine had run out, Mary told Jesus that they were out of wine, and he replied, "What does that have to do with me? It is not yet my time." Jesus reminded Mary that the guests running out of wine wasn't his problem. Jesus had a set time to be revealed as the King of the Jews. The boundary he set with his mom was not to be disrespectful to her, but to honor His timetable to begin His miracle ministry. How many times have we gotten ourselves into a situation when it wasn't really our problem to begin with? We probably could have spared ourselves the pain and frustration if we had just stayed out of it.

Mary, knowing who Jesus was, basically told the waiters to do as he said. Jesus wasn't going to go out of his way to make things happen. He didn't need the wedding guests to know that He was involved at all. He wasn't going to make a big fuss. If the waiters did as he said, He was happy to oblige. So when the waiters brought the water, Jesus did his miracle and turned it into wine. He honored his mother's wishes out of respect for her, but He didn't push himself to be the star of the show or be in the spotlight. He did what he could do to help in the least exposed fashion, and He allowed all the glory to go to the host. As a matter of fact, John is the only gospel in which this story is mentioned. Jesus was able to maintain his boundary of not revealing himself as a miracle worker yet and was able to be helpful and honor the hosts of the wedding feast.

<u>Marriage</u>

Marriage boundaries can seem like a large gray area. This relationship may be the hardest one to set and uphold boundaries, as the majority of marriage experiences aren't black and white and easy to navigate. Within marriage, you experience a mix of love, forgiveness, humility, passion, anger, and volatility. Added to that, you made a vow for better and for worse, in sickness and health, til death do us part that create an array of areas that are covered over in commitment regardless of situations. There is no longer a "mine and yours" in marriage. Now it is "ours." Likes and dislikes, preferences and desires must morph into a unity of one for a marriage to be successful. Working together with your spouse to establish healthy boundaries will show them love in a way they may not even know they needed.

Marriages require sacrificial, firm, and familial boundaries to remain healthy.

Sacrificial boundaries in marriage

Sacrificial boundaries often embody a lot of grace and forgiveness and following where you may not want to go. Sacrificial boundaries are usually practiced in a healthy and safe marriage relationship. After all, none of us are perfect, and we will all need our spouse to give us grace when we mess up. We may hurt their feelings unintentionally, badger them for the same annoying habit, or irritate the fire out of our spouse, but that can fall under grace and forgiveness.

I have a friend whose husband was in the Air Force. He had to move all over the world to uphold his commitment to the military. She followed. She didn't always want to. She had moments that she questioned whether she was going to go, and sometimes it would take months for her to work through her thoughts and feelings about her sacrifice to follow him again. This is when sacrificial boundaries are set in place. She realized that her dedication to him and love for him were worth the releasing of her initial wants because her needs were still being met within the marriage. Their marriage is healthy, reciprocal, and worth navigating complicated situations for.

A spouse that has to move often for a job can cause the other person to give up a lot. The losses in that situation can be a broad spectrum: being away from grown children, not being able to have a steady career, leaving elderly parents behind, not being able to see family and having strong connections to extended family, leaving friends behind, or just not having the stability of a home that they may long for. These are all sacrifices that may be made for the love of another. The ability to work through the feelings that may come along with sacrificial boundaries are similar to the feelings that you will have to work through to have firm boundaries with a spouse.

Firm boundaries in marriage

Firm boundaries are most commonly used when one spouse is an addict or abusive. However, other circumstances may need firm boundaries too. Boundaries are to keep you safe, so set them as you see fit for your situation. Addicted and abusive spouses are not reciprocating love. Many in this situation find themselves practicing sacrificial boundaries when they should be enforcing firm boundaries. Firm boundaries require set consequences for behaviors that cross the set boundary line.

When my late husband had a relapse about a year and half after we married, I had to begin to set some firm boundaries. This situation in 2005 is how I began getting help for myself and understanding boundaries. During this relapse is when I started to attend my Serenity small group. Through the Twelve Steps of Alanon, which are the same steps of Alcoholics Anonymous, I learned to release what I couldn't control but to set firm boundaries with consequences of what I could control. What I did have control over is how much I allowed him to interact with me and our children while he was using. Once I caught him using drugs, and it was no longer just an "accusation" and he could no longer deny it, I made him leave our home. This was the first firm boundary with consequences. It wasn't easy. I had two young children at home.

After about a month of no longer living in the home, he stole some money from me. He wasn't working regularly because he was in an active addiction and was all-consumed by it. He gave me the money from a side job he had done to show me that he was trying to do the right thing and help me, but then he stole it on his way out of the door that night. I was infuriated, disappointed, and devastated. I showed up at the house he was staying at the next morning and told him that he was no longer allowed on the property and he would not be able to pick up the children or be alone with them at any time. If he showed up on my property or at the daycare, the police would be called immediately. This was the next set of firm boundaries with consequences. Jay loved his kids so much. The boundary that he wouldn't be able to see them except for a limited time was enough for him to realize that he needed to go and get help. He signed up for rehab within two–three weeks after that boundary was set.

I couldn't make him go to rehab. I couldn't make him want to get better. I just had to set firm boundaries to protect my children and me from his dangerous behaviors. Anyone mixed in with a drug lifestyle has dangerous behaviors. If you are dealing with an addict, you need to make sure that you are setting boundaries to keep yourself and your children safe. If the person is abusive and an addict, please get support before you set your boundaries with consequences. You will need support and protection. Contact your local YWCA for information.

If you are dealing with someone who is abusive but not an addict, you need to make a game plan to remove yourself and your children safely before you attempt any other steps. Removing yourself and your children will be the firmest boundary that you will set, but it will not be the only boundary. You may need to set the boundary that the abuser has anger management classes and an accountability partner before you will allow any steps towards reconciliation. You do not need to feel obligated to reconcile with someone who has been abusive to you and your children. You are absolutely free to move forward in safety. You do not deserve abuse. Abuse breaks all your vows and all the promises made. The phrase "I'm sorry" doesn't remove the abusive behavior. As I discussed in the forgiveness section in this book, that apology needs to be aligned with changed behavior. Words are not changed behavior. You cannot merely hear words to allow that person back into your intimate space, he/she must do the hard work to regain trust.

Firm boundaries must have consequences connected because that is how humans learn. The boundary is the line you draw for safety around yourself and/or children. The consequences are the actions that come when the boundary is crossed. Once you establish this with your spouse or whomever may need it, you must be willing to uphold the boundary and consequences for them to be effective. My boundary was that Jay couldn't come near us at home or daycare, and the consequence was that the police would be called.

Firm boundaries have their place inside of a non-abusive relationship as well. If you are the spouse paying for all the bills and your spouse spends freely and it harms the family finances, you may have to set a boundary with consequences. The boundary may look like putting a budget into place. If the free spending spouse will not honor the budget, the consequence is separation of finances. The free spending spouse is harming the relationship and trust by not honoring the financial needs of the home. There is only freedom when there is honor and trust in relationships. Without setting the boundary and upholding it and the consequence, the responsible spouse in this scenario is operating out of codependency, which will harm the overall health of the family relationships. The family could end up in substantial debt or financial ruin if the spouses operate out of their issues instead of doing the hard work of setting boundaries.

Firm boundaries can also be set with other family members and relationships that need them, not just specifically for spouses. The interpersonal relationship of marriage is why I am writing about firm boundaries here. Noone is closer than a spouse to throw you off emotionally, mentally, or spiritually, so firm boundaries are usually necessary in an unhealthy marital relationship. This is also the reason that familial boundaries have to be set in marriages.

Familial boundaries

Today our culture seems to struggle with marriage and family boundaries. Parents are staying too engaged and involved in their grown children's lives, and once they are married, it creates chaos. If you grew up in a family without boundaries, you may not even realize that the lack of boundaries is what is causing some of the mess in your marriage. A meddling mother-in-law can be very invasive as well as a father-in-law that is still trying to control. Maybe an out of control sibling is being too needy toward their married sibling and doesn't realize that they are causing issues between the couple. What about the parent that is having to live with the family? That can be a tough situation to set boundaries because there is no separation of living spaces. These scenarios are endless and can be complicated. Boundaries will help lessen the complications.

You *must* set boundaries around your marriage with your spouse so that both of you are on the same page with the extended family. As life changes and situations change, you may have to revisit the boundaries and move the lines as needed, but you do it together. Let's run with the example of the meddling mother-in-law on the husband's side of the family. This mother-in-law gets into every situation the couple has without being asked and without asking if she is welcome. The couple has just bought a new home and the meddling mother-in-law has already criticized the purchase of the home with great exhaustion. She is now purchasing decorations for the new house. She intends to set the garden up in a few weeks. She, also, will have the kitchen painted for them. No need to worry; she has this.

The wife is feeling like she has whiplash, and the husband is silent. He is used to his mom being that way and just accepts it. The wife expresses her dissatisfaction with the invasion, but the husband ignores it, thinking that it's no big deal. This couple will have years of fighting and misery in front of them if they do not stop this cycle.

The best thing the couple can do is to sit together and establish what works for them. They are now the primary unit. Each one can bring their issues to the table and establish what works for them, but once they come to a common ground, the boundary has been set. Meddling mother-in-law is no longer able to create chaos in their marriage because they are working together to uphold the boundary that makes their marriage safe. There may be a fallout from the mother-in-law being upset, but those will ultimately be her issues to work through, and the couple's marriage will be safe regardless of her.

Ultimately, if the couple doesn't set the boundaries, though it may seem hard, the wear and tear on their marriage will be deep and long standing. The lack of boundaries and honoring them is often what can lead a couple to divorce. Remember, boundaries and freedom go hand in hand. Setting boundaries around your marriage to protect it from invasive family members is wise and offers freedom for your marriage to thrive.

Children

Our children can be some of the hardest relational boundaries to set. Why? Because parents feel like they owe the kids, and as a result, the kids often feel like they own the parents. I would dare say that this is a modern-day cultural issue. In past generations, there was a greater divide of authority between parents and their children. There was an understanding, whether natural for the culture or taught, that children had a place of submission to their parents. Today, our culture has it upside down, and many children are running their parents' lives and decisions. This isn't a parenting book, so I won't segue too far off-topic, but I do want to say that if your kids are running your lives and decisions, you have very poor boundaries. You absolutely need to step up and set some healthy boundaries in place so that your children can thrive. Proverbs 13:24, "Whoever spares the *rod* hates their *children*, but the one who loves their *children* is careful to discipline them," is a well-quoted scripture. Many shun this scripture because it seems harsh or people will use it as justification for beating their children, but I think both takes on this scripture are misrepresentations.

The "rod" in scripture is a Hebrew word, and in the Israelite culture, it symbolized authority. In Psalms 23, it says, "Your rod and your staff, they comfort me." So how can "rod" in Proverbs mean to beat your kids and "rod" in Psalms represent comfort? This is one of the issues with translations: not having the cultural context. Most of us don't tend sheep in our modern-day world, so we don't understand that a rod represents safety. The rod was used to fight off predators or anything harmful to the sheep. Our English language is limited in its ability to translate a full language like Hebrew without almost being overly wordy. However, seeking God for revelation as you read the scriptures is the best way to learn what He is really saying and what He means. His word aligns with his character from start to finish, and He will bring light to it. The "rod" representing God's authority is what brings comfort. When we realize that we don't have to control and can't control everything and we have a loving Father whom we can rely on, it is restful. So re-read the Proverbs scripture like this: "Whoever spares their authority over and doesn't protect their children hates their children, but the one who loves their children is careful to discipline them."

With authority and protection come boundaries. There can be no authority or proper protection when there are no boundaries. The Bible encourages parents to show and have authority and protection over their children. That may look different for each family, and I can guarantee that it looks different for each child. Children each are unique and custom-made and fit for you and your ability to have authority. Are they a challenge? Absolutely! Why? Because God put them in your life to stretch, grow, and teach you in ways that no other thing or person or relationship can.

If you begin to establish boundaries with your children at a young age, you will be able to maintain a much healthier relationship. However, no matter what your kids' ages are, it is not too late to start now with boundaries to help begin to heal the broken areas. You may have to start small and work your way up to larger boundaries, and that is OK. Every step in the right direction is the right thing to do. If you need help learning specifics for your circumstances, I would highly recommend finding a group, like Al-Anon or a small group, that can help support you through your journey. Al-Anon can be found online and is a support group to help friends and families of addicts, but it will also help you understand areas where you may have codependent issues that you don't recognize.

Protection is a huge part of this equation. If you do not protect your children from what you can, you are setting them up for some very hard roads ahead. Most drug-addiction issues come from trauma. The addiction is just the outward symptom of a trauma on the inside, like a cough is with a cold. Lack of protection for your children is one of the most dangerous places that parents can find themselves in. What does this look like? It does not look like over-controlling "helicopter parenting." That form of parenting is unhealthy for everyone involved. It does, however, look like a parent willing to ask some hard questions about the kids that are around. It might look like saying no to the sleepover even though your child may not talk to you for a week. It might look like a conversation over questionable thinking that the child has. The scenarios are endless, but as long as that child is a minor and under your authority, protection is important.

I was in a situation not too long ago that was unique for me. I had taken my kids to a friend's house, and earlier in the day when I had talked to the dad, I felt my spirit prompt me to ask if a particular child was there. But I shooed it away thinking, "No, the dad had told me that that kid wasn't allowed back over there." Well, when we showed up, the first person I saw was that kid. My heart sank. I ate pizza and hung out for a bit, and then I got in my car to leave. I brought my son out to the driveway and had a little pep talk with him about this kid and his influence. My son assured me everything was fine. As I pulled out of the driveway, I felt the Holy Spirit say, "Go get your son." I ignored the prompting but questioned it in my head. Then again, the Holy Spirit said, "I gave him to you to protect him. Go get your son." I kept driving. My palms started sweating, which always happens to me when the Spirit is moving with me. I got five minutes down the road and had tried ignoring it, shaking it off, justifying it every which-a-way, but I couldn't do it. I turned around and took my son to the bathroom and told him that I needed him to come home with me.

He said, "But I want to spend the night." I said, "Look. If you will go with me, I'll give you a hundred dollars." Of course, he said OK. But I needed him to know that I was that serious, and for me, it wasn't about the money, though I had asked God what would help motivate him. I could've just told him to do it and he would have, with a lot more guffing and complaining, but my authority stands with my kids, so he would have obeyed me either way. The money was merely me making a point that I needed him to hear. He was receptive and thanked me for protecting him. He asked me later what I thought might happen, and I told him that I didn't know but I was thankful not to have to find out.

I am not telling you to pay your kids $100 to do what you tell them! I was just giving an example in my own life of how the Holy Spirit prompted me to protect my children. It was worth the money because next time I tell him that we are in a hundred-dollar situation, he will know how serious I am and that I need him to heed what I say. The money only backed up the absolute importance of the situation at hand, and it will be the part that he will never forget.

Once you have established your authority and protection over your kids, they will be much more likely to be receptive to your discipline. That is why the next part of the scripture is "The one who loves their children will discipline them." Authority and protection build trust so discipline can take root the way it's meant to. Trying to discipline a child who doesn't trust or respect you only leads to rebellion. So setting the boundaries that lead to healthy authority and healthy protection will also lead to healthy discipline. We are in a broken and fallen world, and things are only going to get worse from here (I'm sorry I don't have better news, but that is what the Bible promises), so we need to do some due diligence as Christians to make sure that we are doing it God's way! It will be harder, and it will take sacrifice because that is the calling of every Christian. The reward, however, will be like none other and will be the greatest thing this side of heaven.

Discipline isn't necessarily an age-defined practice restricted to childhood. God disciplines us throughout our life. He is our heavenly Father and we are his children, no matter how old we get. In the same way, we are always the children of our parents, and we are the parents of our children no matter the age. But as we age, discipline looks less like a time-out or spanking and more like boundaries. We can learn from God how to do that. God might allow us to walk down a really ugly path and make all sorts of bad decisions, and He will just sit there waiting on us to turn around. He doesn't walk down the path with us and try to clean up the messes we make along the way, and He doesn't turn his back and just leave us to our own devices. He will wait, watching, and be there when we decide we have had enough of ourselves. This is how it is to parent an adult child. You can't stop an adult child from doing stupid things, but you don't have to follow them there either. You can just wait and stay steady until they are ready to change their ways. It is absolutely the hardest thing as a parent to relinquish your child to God and just hope that they come out alive. I think that was one of the reasons it was important for Jesus to come and be the propitiation for our sin. God knows what it is like to send His son and let Him go and wait for Him to return. Of course, Jesus didn't do anything wrong, and yet He still had to be fully destroyed and then fully redeemed to save you and me. So God can help you through it. God will lead you and guide you, and with the power of the Holy Spirit, you are able to do it.

Adult-aged children may have a harder time understanding why you are staying still after years of chasing them down dangerous paths or maybe just selfish paths. They may say and do all sorts of nasty things to try and manipulate and control you and guilt you into doing what they want. You will absolutely need support in this case! It will be much harder to do on your own because you are going to have to break old patterns and old boundary lines.

Parents

The Bible says to honor our mother and father so it may go well with you and you will have a long life on this Earth (Exodus 20:12, Ephesians 6:2). This is the first of the Ten Commandments with a promise attached to it. This promise of a long life that is well with you is a good one, especially today! I would like things to go well with me. Honor is defined in the Random House Dictionary of the English Language, 1968, as "1. High public esteem; fame; glory. 2. Honesty or integrity in one's beliefs and actions. 3. A source of credit or distinction . . ." So what does honoring our parents look like? If you have great parents, this may be easy. If you have horrible parents, this may be much, much harder.

Boundaries and Honor with abusive parents

Establishing strong and healthy boundaries with your parents is still important, especially if they are abusive. Parents do not have the right to mistreat you and be hurtful or harmful just because they are your parents.

If you are fully dependent on parents that are emotionally, mentally, or physically abusive to you, remove yourself from the situation as quickly as possible. If you are not able to remove yourself from that situation, I highly recommend finding a group that can help you set strong boundaries and walk through this with you. This may be a great time to do some personal reflection and see what role you have played in this scenario and how you can implement the changes needed to rectify your part of the situation. You are only responsible for your part and what you can control, so do not accept criticisms to the contrary.

Despite their abuse, you can still find ways to honor them. I don't think there is any hidden meaning behind this translation in the Bible. Sometimes, there is contemplation on whether the Bible has a literal or figurative meaning for scriptures. I believe this meaning is exactly what it says it is and meant to be taken exactly as it is meant. Honoring someone who has hurt you in any way takes forgiveness in full. Forgiveness doesn't always mean reconciliation, but in the case of parents, I think that would be ideal if it is possible. There are some instances that it is just not possible and that is OK. God's grace is certainly sufficient for all things.

To honor them, you can help them out. If they need care but are unsafe for you emotionally, mentally, or physically, putting them in a facility that can do the care is OK. If they are still self-sustaining but seem needy of your energy or resources because that is part of their manipulation, you can set a firm calendar and time frames to meet needs without becoming overly committed to spending too much time together. You can also offer to go to counseling with your parent(s) that you are struggling with.

Respect may be shown in not talking badly about a parent. You may think it and feel it, but don't share it with the world. Instead, deliberately take actions to keep negative words and feelings to yourself and, thereby, show your parents honor. You should also talk about the offense without relishing in their punishment and hoping for their destruction. This is where forgiveness in the heart matters so much. I think it is impossible to honor parents without forgiveness for their humanness.

Boundaries and honor with non-abusive parents

I was probably in my thirties when I first realized there were things about my parents that I just didn't like. I had been raised by them, so their "things" were normal to me. Common. However, as I established my own life (I was a late bloomer. Sorry, typical baby of the family here!), I realized they had some personality traits and did things that just irritated the mess out of me. So I began to set boundaries around some of those things. When they made comments that weren't beneficial and even sometimes were hurtful, I set boundaries. When they would "help," but it wasn't really helpful, I set boundaries. For example, my step-dad offered to wash my laundry after my husband passed away. Helpful, right? But he got angry with me when I wasn't able to pick it up from him and he would have to deliver it to me. So I told him not to offer to do the laundry for me anymore. Washing the laundry was helpful but the interaction afterwards was stressful and unnecessary. It would be easier for me to do the laundry myself than to have the emotional drain and strain of dealing with his frustration at me on top of the overwhelming amount of stress I was already enduring.

The ultimate boundaries were set after Jay passed away, and they were intervening too closely with my children. These were the hardest to set because they had always helped me so much with my kids. However, the time had come that their place of helping with my children so intimately was no longer available, and they needed to understand that I had boundaries there. I, ultimately, got into a very heated confrontation with my parents at their house. I packed my children up and left with the intention of not returning until they understood that they can no longer intervene in any way when I am dealing with my children. It wasn't one of my finest moments, but boundaries were established and it has been better ever since. They have been respectful to not cross the line into uninvited grandparent territory and let me parent as I see fit. There may be many moments that you establish new boundaries with your parents and it won't be one specific boundary. Each scenario will require you understanding yourself and how your relationship ebbs and flows. One boundary may require distance. One boundary may require a conversation about respect. One boundary may instill rules for engagement. As for those traits that I just don't like, there is grace. They have to have grace for me, and I have to have grace for them.

One of my favorite stories in the Bible is about Ruth. You can read the Book of Ruth to know it in its entirety. It is a short four-chapter story that is a perfect example of honoring parents. Naomi, her husband, and their two sons moved to Moab. The sons married Moabite women, though they themselves were Hebrews. Naomi lost her husband, and within the next ten years, she lost both of her sons. She had no one to care for her, so she decided to return to Bethlehem to be with her family. Naomi told her two daughters, Ruth and Orpah, to go back to their birth family and gods because she had no other sons to give them and knew that they may be just as desolate along with her once they returned home. Once a woman had married in those days, she no longer belonged to her birth family but to her husband's family. So Naomi was now Ruth's mother and primary loyalty. While Orpah returned to Moab, which is why this story isn't about her, Ruth clung to Naomi and said that Naomi's people and her God would be hers too and that she would not leave her mother unless death parted them.

When they got back to Bethlehem, Naomi told Ruth to go glean (to gather the grains remaining after the regular harvesters) the grain in Boaz's field. He was kind to her, and because of her character and faith, he married her and redeemed her and Naomi. Boaz was Naomi's kinsmen and the great grandfather of David. Oh how God does some amazing things when we honor our parents, including our in-laws!

Ruth could have gone back to her Moabite life and done the familiar thing, the thing she could count on. But she didn't. She did the scary thing and honored Naomi and went with her into an unknown land and into an unknown situation as a foreigner. Honoring Naomi was so important to Ruth that she was willing to have nothing. Because she stepped out in faith and allowed Him to be her God, God gave her honor. Remember the promise that you will have a long life and that it will go well with you? It went well with Ruth. She is in the direct lineage to Christ, and all these thousands of years later, we are still talking about her story. You may never know the impact, this side of heaven, that your willingness to honor your parents has, but one day, in the sweet by and by, God will show you, and you will celebrate the beauty of his goodness.

Ruth's boundaries looked much like sacrifice. Perhaps that is a common theme in honoring parents, but make sure that your boundaries are safe for you mentally, emotionally, and spiritually. Some boundaries are set by what you allow to stay in. Boundaries are not always about keeping things out. Just like we mentioned when we were talking about how houses are boundaries, what we allow to stay inside may fall in the area of sacrificial boundaries. We sacrifice opinions, attitudes, and preferences for people that we love so that we can maintain healthy relationships with the people we have in our close space. Marriage, children and parent relationships may, at times, require sacrificial boundaries.

Interdependence is the goal

Our relationships consist of dependence, independence, or interdependence. Depending on what level of emotional maturity one has, a person will be able to move through the steps of dependence (childhood), to independence (adulthood), to interdependence (marriage and other relationships). The goal is to attain interdependence without codependency in all relationships one experiences.

Dependence is when one person is unable to provide, to function, to think, and/or to sustain themselves. Children are dependents. They are the best example of healthy dependents until the age they should be independent of their parents. But we know that the transition from dependent to independent does not happen overnight and may be a messy, irregular process. An unhealthy example of dependence is a spouse that is unable to function individually and is a consumer of the other spouse's mental, emotional, and physical abilities; these people will also tend to be codependent. Their codependency is reliant on the other person because they are unable to stand alone in any area or most areas. The blame game and victim mentality will be strong with dependent individuals. They rarely, maybe never, will take responsibility for anything because they have become a parasite on another and often look to that individual as the beginning and end of everything that goes right or wrong in their lives.

Independence is a natural and healthy growth step into adulthood. Independent people are entirely self-sufficient with life's demands. This is a good thing until it creates harm in a relationship by not allowing the space for sacrificial boundaries that may be needed in a relationship. An unhealthy independent relationship is when two or more people (i.e. parents working with a grown child) need to work together, but each person is unwilling to change or set healthy boundaries so that each person is able to contribute to the relationship and feel more included. There may be many quarrels in relationships with people who are very independent. Independent people may also be codependent; controlling, typically, but enabling is also a possibility.

Independence healthily grows into interdependence as our relationships grow to be more in depth, like in marriage. Two independent people merging together to create an interdependent relationship is ideal. Interdependence is when people work functionally well within relationships.

Interdependent relationships are when boundaries are set and each person is able to feel safe within the operations of the other person's boundaries. There is a synchronicity in interdependent relationships that allow each person to thrive. When interdependence is operating in a family or workplace, usually there is a system (how each person operates effectively) and an understanding of each person. There is a healthy consideration of the wants, needs and desires of each person, and they are being met within the safety boundary lines. Interdependent relationships have balance. Provision, functionality, thought processes and sustenance are balanced by all parties being involved in their role and part of each life situation with cohesiveness. Codependency has no place inside interdependent relationships. The goal of healthy relationships is finding interdependent balance by using boundaries.

Actionable Items:

As a family member:
- List three family situations where you haven't set proper boundaries. What were the results? List three family situations where you had healthy boundaries in place. What were the results?
- Write down your child(ren)'s name(s). Do you have a healthy relationship with them? Where could boundaries help?
- Write down your parents' names. Do you have a healthy relationship with them? Where could boundaries help?

As an employee:
- What situations have gone poorly at work that you were involved in? What was your responsibility in the situation?
- List one to three boundaries that may have been helpful in that situation.
- For example, your coworker and you were gossiping. You realize that it is unhealthy and hurtful behavior, so you tell your coworker that you can't participate in the conversation anymore.

As a boss:
- Take an inventory of your business policies. These are boundaries set into place for business culture.
- Are you upholding these policies?
- Do they align with your business culture?

Visit my website for more information and ideas!

Chapter 11

Church Culture and Faith Practices

Why do we need boundaries for church culture and faith practices? Because church hurt is a real thing and a real issue today. Religious practices, as far back as the beginning of the established Law of Moses in Exodus, have been hard on humans. The Law isn't bad; we just can't keep it. So God sent Jesus to fulfill it all for us and let us live in the place of grace. Still to this day, when churches stand on Law practices, they tend to hurt more people than they help. Shame, condemnation, and guilt play on the human psyche like a parasite, and it all stems from an unhealthy relationship with the people and/or practices that we sometimes trust to speak into our lives.

Boundaries in all relationships are important, but setting boundaries as to who speaks into your life is just as important. The power people have is only what we give them. Boundaries help us give them the correct amount of power and direct it in the correct place. The boundaries will protect you from being taken advantage of and from potentially throwing you into a place of church hurt and church rebellion.

If you have church hurt, it is still important to go to church. Gathering together with our brothers and sisters is a biblical principle, as shared in Hebrews 10:25. We empower each other when we are together, and God says where two or more are gathered together in my name, He is there in the midst of us (Matthew 18:20). *Ecclesia*, the church, as referenced in the Bible, is Greek for "meeting of the summoned ones" and is part of the purpose of Jesus' coming. He tells Peter that he would be the rock on which the church was built. The church is the people who comprise the body of Christ, not the meeting place where the people gather. That is, the church is not a building where you attend a gathering. Often we say that we are "going to church," but truly we *are* the church. Where there are people, there is sin; and where there is sin, there is hurt; and where there is hurt, there is animosity and resentment, but we must cover it in the blood of forgiveness and grace and set healthy boundaries needed to be the healthiest church we can be.

Don't put church leadership on a pedestal

When church leadership is not held accountable for their actions and behaviors, it can be very damaging for the people who have entrusted them. However, sometimes when a pastor or a person in leadership gets "caught" doing something wrong, it can be the most freeing moment for the pastor because then they can be completely honest and any "holier than thou" posturing will have been destroyed anyway. Years ago a very prominent pastor had been caught having an affair. It, of course, did the damage that you'd expect: Christians everywhere were angry, and his church congregation took a huge blow. But for me, I was relieved and happy for him. See, because we are meant to worship, we will always put something on a pedestal and so many people will put pastors in the place of being worshiped. People will make them idols. This is why you are seeing the generations of "rock star" pastors who seem like celebrities. But by putting them on a pedestal, we are devastated when they come crashing down because they remind us that they are . . . gasp . . . wait for it . . . *human*. The day this prominent pastor came clean was the first time in who knows how many years that he was able to be real before himself and God. Was God surprised? Nope. God was just waiting on him to be able to deal with the sin in his life, and God knew that as long as the pastor had been put in God's rightful place, the man's pride would prevent him from getting real with himself. We are not demigods and we cannot handle the idolization or worship of others. We will always crush under that weight.

If you currently, or have in the past, put humans in the place of being worshiped in your life and have ended up hurt, you can change your direction from here and begin to set boundaries for yourself. Your boundaries may look like visiting a different church every Sunday for a little while, while you get out of a habit or routine of sitting under the same pastor regularly. This will open your eyes up to other teachings and will help you broaden your perspective of how other churches operate. You may even try to really step out of your comfort zone and try other ethnicities and denominations so you can see that God has a broad brush stroke of people and ways to worship and love Him. Pray that God will open himself up to you so you are worshiping Him alone. Read your Bible. Reading the Bible is like grilling time with God.

I don't know about you, but where I live, we love to grill out. It is warm here in the South most of the year, so usually we can grill year-round. After our coldest months, February to April usually, we look forward to the nice spring days and invite friends over and grill. It is a time of fellowship, fun, and food— three of my favorite things in the world. I don't think it is a coincidence that a feast will be one of our first experiences in heaven. I can't wait!! The more I experience the fellowship, fun, and food with people, the closer I am to them. We have memories and feel bonded. That is what reading the Bible will do with you and God. Bring some food or coffee and settle in and get to know your heavenly Father. If you find the Bible to be boring, pray before you start:

Lord, please open your Word to me and let my spirit receive what my mind may not be capable of yet. You promise that your word will not return void, so I ask that you help me to receive what I need to. I want to hang out with you and get to know you.
In Jesus' name,
Amen.

It's a simple little prayer like that can change your experience. You are opening yourself up to receive all God has for you and He will meet you there. He loves to hang out with us. "He delights in us," is what the Bible tells us. Have you ever walked into a room and seen someone you know and he or she smiles? I think that is how God feels when we sit down and open His Word and spend time with Him.

<u>Confusing Christianity</u>

Christianity is based on the fundamental idea that an absolute truth exists outside of the "truth" that surrounds us every day. We believe that God sent His only son to be the sacrifice and atonement for our sins and to conquer Death and Hades, and that after three days, He rose again out of the grave and walked the Earth, then ascended into heaven, and is now there as our advocate. We believe that when we die, we join with Jesus, and one day we will all be in heaven together after Judgment Day.

It sounds crazy, right? Like who in their right mind would follow a deity that calls for the sacrifice of His own son? Why in the world would He just not make him the King and have everyone worship Him and it all be glamorous and spectacular? Why would He send his Godhead son as a baby just to grow up and be killed in a horrific way?

Because we matter that much. Because God loved the world so much that He sent His only son that whoever believes in Him will have eternal life, and He did not send His Son to judge the world but that it might be saved through Him (John 3:16–17) Because God has standards that are set and those standards required the best to atone the wrath of sin. Because sin is that deadly and that awful. Make no mistake that God has serious boundaries about sin, and it not being acceptable: Proverbs 8:13, Proverbs 6:16–19, Romans 6:23 are just a few scriptures to support my point but really the whole entire Bible, beginning with the Fall of Man in the Garden of Eden, supports the notion that God detests sin and requires holiness for his followers.

Apparently, we have a modern-day concept that everything in the Bible is up to subjective thinking. I find this to be the most dangerous form of "Christianity" out there, and it is mostly what makes Christians seem hypocritical. I mean, if we can't even agree on what the absolute truth is, then is there even an absolute truth? Yes. There is an absolute truth. The truth is sin exists, it is deadly to our hearts, minds, and bodies, and we do not get to set what that truth is, God does. This is one of His firmest boundaries. God and evil are adversaries and immiscible. They cannot reside in the same place. The Bible tells us that we cannot serve two masters, that we will despise one and love the other. So we cannot simultaneously be doing whatever we want and whatever feels right to us and follow the ways of God. I mean, if Jesus had to be sacrificed for an atonement of sin, that should give you an idea of the level of separation needed from sin and your life. God doesn't allow us to be tempted in any way that He doesn't make a way out of. 1 Corinthians 10:13 is the promise that we won't be tempted more than we can handle, and if we do face that position, God has made a way out of it.

We will face temptation and sin. Our flesh and its tendencies are not in line with God and His ways because of sin. Will Saints sin? Yes, the difference between being a saint who sins and a sinner who claims to be Christian is the purity of heart. A saint will indeed sin because we are prone to that behavior, but repentance and true acknowledgement will be close and we will work toward a change in behavior and a change in our person. A sinner who claims Christianity will do whatever they want to do and use the Bible to justify their behavior and continue to do whatever they want to do. We see this concept in Titus 1:

[15] To the pure, all things are pure, but to the defiled and unbelieving, nothing is pure; but both their minds and their consciences are defiled. [16] They profess to know God, but they deny Him by their works. They are detestable, disobedient, unfit for any good work. (ESV)

This is confusing Christianity.

We will never have uniformity in Christianity because God never wanted us to be robots, but there is a standard by which we should be known: 1) the fruits of our Spirit—love, joy, peace, perseverance, kindness, goodness, faithfulness (Galatians 5:22–23)—2) to be above reproach (blameless) if we are an elder or leader in ministry (Titus 1:5–9), 3) we are holy and set apart (Romans 12:2, 1 Peter 2:9).

God made us all with an array of personalities and of thinking processes, but we make ourselves god when we use these traits He gave us to usurp His standards and His ways. We cannot justify sinful lifestyles and sinful behaviors so we can feel better about sinning.

Unfortunately today, there seems to be a lot of hypocrisy in this area, too. A divorcée will look down on someone who is living with their significant other or a person prone to fighting will think that they are better than someone who doesn't fight, or neighbors will be unkind to neighbors because an animal pooped in the yard, and yet they spout Christian values. All these kinds of things are hypocritical and you will find that they do not align with the fruits of the Spirit or the standards that God has set into place. When we fail to see how our own pride gets us into so much trouble, we fail to see the log in our own eye while we try to remove the splinter out of their eye (Matthew 7:5). All sin is destructive, and we are the only ones who put weights and measurements on sin, not God.

Hebrews 10:26 tells us that once we have the knowledge of truth, if we continue to sin, then we no longer have a sacrifice for our sins. See, our sacrifice covers our ignorance of sin. Before we knew Jesus, we didn't have an acknowledgement of sin.

Paul talks about this struggle in Romans 7. He discusses not knowing what sin was until the Law told him. Once the Law made him aware of sin, he was all the more prone to continue doing it. Just like when someone says, "Don't look at that woman over there but . . ." and the first thing you do is look. That is our nature. We are told not to do something and then find ourselves doing that very thing. Maybe out of rebellion. Maybe out of pure curiosity. I love Paul's raw honesty in this passage because he states the human condition so well. We didn't know it was sin until we were told it was sin. Thus when someone isn't a believer, they don't understand sin. They most likely experience sin and its painful and negative effects, but they don't know how to change it or move away from it or have the power to abstain or get away from sin.

Jesus, while on the cross, said, "Forgive them, Father. They don't know what they are doing." I believe this was his first plea as our advocate while He took our sin onto His back. He was willing to carry our weight when we were ignorant and didn't know how to be/do anything differently. Once we become His brothers and sisters, once we know His grace and harness the power of the Holy Spirit, we no longer sin in ignorance but by choice and that doesn't fall under grace. It would make it easy if it did, wouldn't it? It would be easy to just continue to do whatever we want and justify it or let it fall under grace. We are called to love God and keep his commandments (1 John 5:3, John 14:15)

Don't fool yourself into thinking that you are a listener when you are anything but, letting the Word go in one ear and out the other. Act on what you hear! Those who hear and don't act are like those who glance in the mirror, walk away, and two minutes later have no idea who they are, what they look like. (James 1:22–24 in The Message translation)

Thus, if you are not turning from your sin and continuing to walk in whatever way you want, you are fooling yourself and confusing your Christianity. There is an absolute truth. There is a loving, Holy, and just God that stands on this truth for our benefit. He made sure we have every avenue necessary to be rescued from ourselves. Use all the tools He gave you and do not struggle with confusing Christianity. If you are questioning your salvation, then you may want to "grill out" with God more so He can reveal himself to you and allow His light to shine in your life. I promise you that it will not be easy to shed hardcore sin lifestyles, but it is possible. I promise you that turning away from sin will be the best thing that has happened to you. I promise you that you will never regret giving God your all.

If you do not set boundaries around your beliefs and know that you know that you believe in God's Word, you may find yourself succumbing to confusing Christianity. It is a slippery slope in today's culture of faith practices to just do what feels good. Setting boundaries for yourself about your wisdom and knowledge of God will protect you when you face a situation that may be confusing or calling for compromise. Trust God. Follow Him.

Judging others

My boundary with salvation is to let that be up to God. I do not judge others' salvation nor should you. We are not God. He is very specific that sin separates.

Saints need to be very careful with judging others and holding court here on Earth for God. Matthew 7:2 is a great warning for those who want to judge others. "Do not judge . . ." is the very beginning of this scripture commanding Saints not to judge. If Jesus wasn't sent to judge the world (John 3:17), then what in the world makes us think that God wants us in that role? Then Matthew goes on to explain that if you choose to judge, you will be judged in exactly the same way, and the extent of the measure of condemnation you use will be used against you. Holding others accountable to the standards by which they, themselves, set is not judging. Holding others accountable to standards that they do not claim but you want to enforce upon them is judging.

You cannot expect a non-believer to act or think or behave like a believer in Christ. You cannot expect someone who doesn't believe in Jesus to practice Christian principles or faith practices. You can ask them to be respectful as you do, but they may—and probably will—decline to participate. This is not a time to shun them or push them away, but to share what Jesus has done for you. There is power in our testimony (Revelation 12:11, Acts 4:33). Tell your testimony, but live at peace with those who do not believe as much as you possibly can. The Message Bible translation of this principle in Romans 14: 1–23 is perfect for better understanding.

Welcome with open arms fellow believers who don't see things the way you do. And don't jump all over them every time they do or say something you don't agree with—even when it seems that they are strong on opinions but weak in the faith department. Remember, they have their own history to deal with. Treat them gently.

2-4 For instance, a person who has been around for a while might well be convinced that he can eat anything on the table, while another, with a different background, might assume he should only be a vegetarian and eat accordingly. But since both are guests at Christ's table, wouldn't it be terribly rude if they fell to criticizing what the other ate or didn't eat? God, after all, invited them both to the table. Do you have any business crossing people off the guest list or interfering with God's welcome? If there are corrections to be made or manners to be learned, God can handle that without your help.

5 Or, say, one person thinks that some days should be set aside as holy and another thinks that each day is pretty much like any other. There are good reasons either way. So, each person is free to follow the convictions of conscience.

6-9 What's important in all this is that if you keep a holy day, keep it for God's sake; if you eat meat, eat it to the glory of God and thank God for prime rib; if you're a vegetarian, eat vegetables to the glory of God and thank God for broccoli. None of us are permitted to insist on our own way in these matters. It's God we are answerable to—all the way from life to death and everything in between—not each other. That's why Jesus lived and died and then lived again: so that he could be our Master across the entire range of life and death, and free us from the petty tyrannies of each other.

10-12 So where does that leave you when you criticize a brother? And where does that leave you when you condescend to a sister?

I'd say it leaves you looking pretty silly—or worse. Eventually, we're all going to end up kneeling side by side in the place of judgment, facing God. Your critical and condescending ways aren't going to improve your position there one bit. Read it for yourself in Scripture:

"As I live and breathe," God says,
"every knee will bow before me;
Every tongue will tell the honest truth
that I and only I am God."

So mind your own business. You've got your hands full just taking care of your own life before God.

13-14 Forget about deciding what's right for each other. Here's what you need to be concerned about: that you don't get in the way of someone else, making life more difficult than it already is. I'm convinced—Jesus convinced me!—that everything as it is in itself is holy. We, of course, by the way we treat it or talk about it, can contaminate it.

15-16 If you confuse others by making a big issue over what they eat or don't eat, you're no longer a companion with them in love, are you? These, remember, are persons for whom Christ died. Would you risk sending them to hell over an item in their diet? Don't you dare let a piece of God-blessed food become an occasion of soul-poisoning!

17-18 God's kingdom isn't a matter of what you put in your stomach, for goodness' sake. It's what God does with your life as he sets it right, puts it together, and completes it with joy. Your task is to single-mindedly serve Christ. Do that and you'll kill two birds with one stone: pleasing the God above you and proving your worth to the people around you.

[19-21] So let's agree to use all our energy in getting along with each other. Help others with encouraging words; don't drag them down by finding fault. You're certainly not going to permit an argument over what is served or not served at supper to wreck God's work among you, are you? I said it before and I'll say it again: All food is good, but it can turn bad if you use it badly, if you use it to trip others up and send them sprawling. When you sit down to a meal, your primary concern should not be to feed your own face but to share the life of Jesus. So be sensitive and courteous to the others who are eating. Don't eat or say or do things that might interfere with the free exchange of love.

[22-23] Cultivate your own relationship with God, but don't impose it on others. You're fortunate if your behavior and your belief are coherent. But if you're not sure, if you notice that you are acting in ways inconsistent with what you believe—some days trying to impose your opinions on others, other days just trying to please them—then you know that you're out of line. If the way you live isn't consistent with what you believe, then it's wrong."

As far as sin behaviors and judging go, I dare say to be very careful, Saint. You are not walking their walk. It is their walk with God, and all you can do is encourage them and speak truth in love. But you can stand on truth as you do so. Like we talked about with some cultural boundaries, you do not have to be bullied into agreeing with others and their choices and lifestyles just because others think you should. You can always choose to remain silent if it is the best option. Do not allow Christians to bully you into being loud about topics of their convictions either, be it political or personal. These situations are OK to have some strong boundaries and to protect yourself and your own walk as needed. In some seasons in your life, you may plug in and then in other seasons, you need to walk away.

The way, the truth, and the life

Jesus is the way, the truth, and the life, and no one can come to the Father except through Him (John 14:6–7). Jesus, then, is a boundary God set into place. It is the boundary where grace meets the human race. There is no leeway, there is no exception, and there is no side door. Jesus, including His life and His mission, is the only example of God-made flesh on this Earth that we have. In that same passage of John, Jesus shares with us that to know Him is to know the Father and vice versa.

Universalism goes against that biblical passage and may create confusion for you if you aren't setting your boundaries according to truth. Universalism will tell you that surely there has to be other ways. This is because Universalism regards Jesus as a worthy teacher and prophet but in no way divine.

Universalism thinks: What happens to all the people who have never heard of or don't believe in Jesus? How can a loving God send those people to hell? He wouldn't, so they have to go to heaven. Or they think, I don't even believe in hell. Heaven is just a theory and there is no hell. These are just figurative places in the Bible.

Universalism feels good to us. It says that everyone will be able to make it and that there is no place for a loving God to withhold from his children. God is loving, but that is only one part of Him. You can't remove the uncomfortable parts about Him and still know him fully. Anytime you remove the unsavory parts of a relationship, you are fooling yourself and not recognizing the fullness of the relationship or of the person. If you have ever been in any sort of long-term relationship, you understand this concept, especially in marriage. You don't stay married to someone because they are perfect and awesome all the time. That isn't real. You stay in the relationship because you know there is value to the relationship and that even at the other person's worst, they are amazing. Even though the other person has some traits that you may not like and that may drive you nuts, you love them fully and accept that their flaws aren't the entirety of them.

Now, don't mistake God's holiness, justice, and hatred of sin as "negative" traits to be tolerated. These traits are just as beautiful as his love, grace, and mercy. They are all-encompassing of a *huge* God with vastness that our human minds cannot comprehend. I just wanted to use the limited understanding of our human relationships as a comparison so we can see that sometimes we must accept things about God that we may not personally like or understand so we can live in the truth of who He is and not who we want Him to be.

There is no place for Universalism and Christianity to coexist. One is a lie. There is either absolute truth that Jesus is the only way or it is a lie. It cannot be kind of true; Jesus cannot be kind of divine. It cannot be slightly true; Jesus cannot be slightly divine, a demi-god of sorts. Jesus staked his life on it.

In order to protect your religious convictions, you need to set the boundary that you will not be swayed by half-truths that make humans feel better. You must accept God and Jesus as they are.

There are many other religions in this world. Some are interesting and seem so good. But Christianity isn't solely a religion. It is a relationship. You cannot earn it. You cannot buy it. You cannot bargain for it. The relationship through salvation is a gift freely given to those who choose to accept it. If I am given a car but continue to walk, what good does the car do for me? I must use the car so that its potential is reached and understood. If I have always walked and never driven, I would probably be quite afraid of driving for the first time. I might even be afraid of getting in the car at all.

Could I trust this machine?
Could I trust myself with it?
How does it work?
Why change to a car when walking has worked just fine all these years?
I don't think I even need a car.

These are all valid questions and statements. You are right. You could continue to walk for the rest of your life and probably do everything you have needed to do by the limitations of walking. But! But what if? What if you give the car a chance? What if you trust the machine and trust yourself and turn that key and get those four wheels rolling. Now it all comes together and you understand the beauty of driving! You can now go farther, faster, and more efficiently than you could before. You can get your groceries and more of them because you are not limited by your own capacity but now have the full capacity of your car. You can carry friends and family places. You can now carry gifts to those who are farther than your legs could have carried you. You now have power you never had before.

This is how a relationship with Jesus works. It can be super scary if you've never done it before. It can be super scary when you have never been loved, to think someone you can't touch and can't see, can love you so deeply and that you are in an active relationship. Weird, huh?! But once you experience the intimacy of Jesus and the complete love of God the Father and the power of the Holy Spirit, there is nothing better!

Your relationship will take off and all the hesitation and reservations will cease as you grill out with God by reading your Bible and spending time in prayer, which is our ultimate intimacy with God.

The church and politics

The Church has hurt itself more times than it may be able to count by getting involved with politics. This is a root that has been growing since the very first centuries of church establishment and even in cultures that we can't understand today. For instance, kings and bishops were intertwined, and the Church often established the relevancy of the king to the point that the Church could destroy a King.

Kings would force their belief systems on their people, whether they were for the Christian God or not. We see many examples throughout the Bible of kings who worshiped Baal and other gods. In Daniel, we see a powerful representation of when the Israelites had been taken captive and brought to Babylon to serve as slaves. Their Hebrew names were changed, and they were required to indulge in the king's luxuries and were expected to adopt the culture and gods of the Babylonians. Daniel (meaning "God is my judge") was given the name Belteshazzar (meaning masculine "the keeper of secrets"). Daniel, though given a new name, did not sway from what he knew was right and true and continued to follow his God, the God of the Hebrews. It is a fascinating story, and I suggest you take some time to read it, and even do a Bible study on it.

Daniel wasn't going to allow his place or his circumstances to change what he knew to be true. He would not turn away from God. He set boundaries around what he would do and, at the same time, submitted to the authority over him. It is a beautiful picture of how God can always bring honor to the one who follows Him when everything about the circumstance says that it is impossible.

We don't have kings running the show anymore. We have politicians, who I dare say think they are kings. The government shouldn't be regulating others' morality, and the government shouldn't be forcing others to support things the people find immoral. When the government steps in, there is often an overreach. But, Christians, you can't have it both ways. You can't regulate morality for others and then expect them not to want you to be forced in the other direction. This is the major issue with the conflation of church and politics. It is solely the church's responsibility to encourage the morality of others with the truth in love. When the church steps in and tries to regulate morality with laws, the church really looks like the overreaching fool. This is the church establishing morality for others based on its own moral principles. God is the One that does the heart work in others. He is really good at it, and we can trust that He will do the work in others if we show them the way to Him and live a life that sets a good example.

If you let your political beliefs sour a relationship by regulating someone else's morality and political beliefs, then you are letting your political ideologies outshine Jesus. Jesus is not present where there is no love. You need to set a boundary that the love of Jesus will always be first and foremost in your interactions with non-believers or those of differing political opinions.

Where I live, there is a very large church that has way too much say in the goings-on of the city. They have prevented restaurants, movie theaters, family entertainment, and other beneficial revenue from coming here because they want everyone to adhere to their morality. As a believer, I am totally put off by their invasive draconian actions. They suffocate and stifle community growth by their own limitations and oppress the rest of us with it. They would probably say that it is "moral" to do this, but when did they become the judge for others? This is the same sort of conflation that the early church had with kings. There was a sick marriage that happened that was never meant to be.

Remember, according to scripture, we are the *bride of Christ*, not the bride of this Earth or the kings of this Earth. Our main objective is to keep ourselves unstained by this world (James 1:27) and to love God with all of our heart, soul, and mind and to love our neighbors as ourselves (Matthew 22:37–39). We can set boundaries around what is best for us, but we cannot get so deep into the political pool that we drown out our genuine purpose.

The most recent example of this is the situation with Christians, especially Evangelicals, and former President Trump. I am not saying whether you should be for or against him. I am indifferent to your political beliefs, so bear with me. In this last election, a line was crossed with the Christian political stances and the former president. It seemed from many outside perspectives that the Christians treated him like a savior. This, in turn, tarnished the perception of Christians by many non-believers outside of the church. My question to you is simply this: Did Jesus shine in this?

Anytime, we put any politician or political figure in the place of Christ, we are standing on quicksand and in a very dangerous place. Do we get the chance to have our voices heard? Yes! Absolutely, share your voice, but don't let your voice squish others to the point of losing your Jesus voice. There will never be a point in humanity when everyone agrees with each other. It's what makes humanity unique, and as I stated earlier, these are all God-created personalities, fellow image-bearers. Sharing your voice and standing firm for what you believe personally is a beautiful act of worship toward God when He is leading it. Trying to force others to think the same way gets into a danger zone that the world has always experienced and always bucked. So set a clear boundary that you will stand firm in your beliefs, but also set the boundary that you will not cross the line into forcing others to think like you.

Well, Stephanie, does that just mean we sit back and let our country "go to hell in a handbasket"? NO! It means to be prayer warriors! Prayer is one of the most powerful tools that we can wield. You best believe that things on Earth are moved when we pray and when we trust and believe in our God. It means to be diligent in your own lives! The more diligent you are and purposeful in your own lives, the greater influence you have on those around you. Be the person that others desire to be like, so when they have the chance to share their voice, it shines Jesus. It means setting healthy boundaries so that you are in healthy relationships and can make healthy decisions that aren't full of manipulations and confusion. Please vote! Please let your voice be heard. Engage in your local political happenings and be a light and voice for Christ. Your role is important there. But remember your role is to shine Christ, not yourself.

We, Christians, aren't looking for moral law abiders. We are looking for brothers and sisters in Christ to share eternity with and build the Kingdom of God on Earth. When we excel in this area, that is when we change the world!

Actionable Items:

- Which church(es) have you experienced church hurt? Pray for a forgiving heart toward that church.
- If you hold any church leader on a pedestal, release them from that position of worship and recognize they are human.
- Ask yourself if you have been swayed by half-truths. If yes, develop a scripture-based prayer that will help you.
- If your political beliefs have outshined Jesus, list three ways you can show Christ first to those in your realm of influence.

Part three:

Putting it into action

Chapter 12

The Journey

I told you a little about my journey at the beginning of this book. My Heartship was a total wreck. I came into adulthood and didn't know anything about boundaries and why they were important. Having lost my father at the tender age of four, I was on a lifelong journey of seeking to fill the hole he had left deep inside of me. In order to fill that hole, I had given my heart away wastefully more times than I care to count. I kept getting tripped up on a false sense of love. It was a "me and you against the world" idea of love that led me down foolish paths. I knew God, but I didn't realize the fullness of God. I didn't realize that what I was looking to fill my heart with was right there all along. I just needed to put the puzzle pieces in the right place, but I didn't know that I had all the pieces there already. You have all the pieces too if you have asked Jesus to become the Lord of your life. You have all the pieces to fill the empty places in your life and illuminate the way to health and wholeness within your heart.

Once I began to trust the process of setting boundaries, it has become easier and easier to do. It was super scary at first because I didn't want others to feel like I was rejecting them, and I didn't want to be rejected either. Some relationships grow deep roots that are like kudzu (an introduced vine plant that has literally taken over the South). It seems like you are in too deep to ever get free. Sweet child of God, that is a lie! Jesus came and died for your freedom. It is yours. You just have to take the right next step. You just have to start in one place, and then diligently keep walking forward. Your one step today may just be starting to pray for wisdom on how to do the next step. But you keep praying that prayer! Pray it every day, and when the door to the next step arrives, take that step. Step through that door. Do not be afraid!

Fear

Fear is a liar and will hold you captive for as long as you will let it. If you let it, it will keep you from creating and enforcing your boundaries. You may fear hurting the other person, you may fear that you will be seen as mean, and you may fear that your boundaries will leave you as the odd one out in this modern world, but you need to break out of that fear. When you try to break free from fear, it will scream louder and the threats will become greater, but the truth is that God did not give you a spirit of fear but of power, love, and sound mind (2 Timothy 1:7). When your spirit is awakened with power from the Holy Spirit, you will be able to overcome fear. It may take some practice, but you can do it.

You may wonder why I say it'll take practice, but the spirit of fear is real. It is like being in a cave of darkness with threats on all sides. You feel too scared to move because any direction you go threatens to be the wrong decision. Let me just tell you that you may stumble and fall and it may hurt, and you may feel beat up and scarred on your way out, especially depending on how far you've allowed yourself to go into the cave, but one step toward the exit is worth it because once you are free, life will change and become an entirely new experience. You are meant to be a beacon of light! In Luke 11:33, the Bible explains that no one lights a lamp and then puts it under a basket or in the cellar. In our modern age, I would extend this to say that no one would install a light bulb under a couch. The illumination is meant to guide and lead you, and you, Believer, are a light of God to this world. You are meant to shine. Fear may steal that away from you as long as you let it. It will try to snuff out the light in you, but it only has the power that you give it. There is no power in fear itself. The only seeming power is deception, like any spiritually dark force. If fear has hidden your light, your light still is shining and waiting to be welcomed out of the darkness. Use your inner light to find your way out of that cave!

A lot of the time, fear is the propelling force behind our bad decisions and situations that get us into bad places. Fear of never being loved will potentially put you in a relationship that is abusive and sick. But you hold on because no one else will love you and you would rather have something bad than nothing at all. This is a lie. It is better to be alone than to be in an abusive relationship. You can find someone to love you when you are healthy in mind and looking for someone who is also healthy. And to get there, it all starts with boundaries. It may not happen right away, but you will find healthy relationships. But you do already have one healthy relationship: you are loved by the Almighty God, and He will move mountains to be in a relationship with you. He will fill you from the inside; your heart and mind and body will be stable and secure so you will be OK standing on your own. When the lies that come against you tell you that you haven't changed and that you are still the same, you will be able to destroy them with the truth of how God has healed you.

The fear of facing the bad things that happened to us in childhood often leads to drug use and addiction. We feel like we are being in control because we are numbing ourselves to our feelings, and this creates a delusion that things aren't that bad, but the truth is that we are totally wrecking everything around us by being out of control. Instead, we should face the fear with God as our guide. There is no devastation that can't be healed if we allow the Great Physician to guide us. It won't be easy, but it will bring us out of the fear. This fear is multi-level because some of the fear stems from it happening again, or from how it made us feel inside (like dirty or shameful), and the fear of not being rescued. As these fears grow with us into adulthood, the drowning out of the fear with numbing chemicals is most important in our minds and the most dangerous for our lives and futures.

Fear of not having control can lead to all sorts of addictive-like behaviors or anger issues. These behaviors can consist of obsessive thinking, physical abuse, micromanaging, cutting/self-harm, fits of rage, and not caring what happens to your physical body (being reckless). If we are honest, none of us has control. When could you ever stop or prevent something from happening? The idea of being able to control a situation to your benefit is manipulation, especially if it involves other humans. If you think you controlled a situation, you probably faced consequences for your interference. I think about the Nancy Kerrigan and Tonya Harding situation in January 1994. They were both on the stage to win a championship, but Tonya Harding wanted to get rid of her competition, so she hurt Nancy Kerrigan really badly. She wanted to retain control because the fear of losing clouded her judgment. Did it work out for her? Nope! Tonya Harding not only ended up without the championship, but her reputation was tarnished and destroyed, she lost the respect that she did have, and she faced criminal charges. Often we try to control something that we truly have little or no control over because of a lack of healthy boundaries. We end up in a worse situation and potentially really harm ourselves and others.

Fear of not having enough, being poor, or lacking something can create destructive behaviors like selling drugs, stealing, and hoarding. I know what it is like to be scrounging in life. It is awful and makes things so hard and often tiring. There is no such thing as easy in adulthood. You must do the hard things and you must rest on God. The fear of lacking something isn't a new concept. Matthew records Jesus speaking about it during his ministry in Matthew 6:25–34:

> *25 For this reason I say to you, do not be worried about your ¹life, as to what you will eat or what you will drink; nor for your body, as to what you will put on. Is life not more than food, and the body more than clothing? 26 Look at the birds of the sky, that they do not sow, nor reap, nor gather crops into barns, and yet your heavenly Father feeds them. Are you not much more important than they? 27 And which of you by worrying can add a single day to his life's span? 28 And why are you worried about clothing? Notice how the lilies of the field grow; they do not labor nor do they spin thread for cloth, 29 yet I say to you that not even Solomon in all*

his glory clothed himself like one of these. ³⁰ But if God so clothes the grass of the field, which is alive today and tomorrow is thrown into the furnace, will He not clothe you much more? You of little faith! ³¹ *Do not worry then, saying, "What are we to eat?" or "What are we to drink?" or "What are we going to wear for clothing?" ³² For the Gentiles eagerly seek all these things; for your heavenly Father knows that you need all these things. ³³ But seek first His kingdom and His righteousness, and all these things will be provided to you. ³⁴ So do not worry about tomorrow; for tomorrow will worry about itself. Each day has enough trouble of its own. (NASB)*

Despite a fear of lacking, I found in my own life that when I started tithing, God began to open up the flow of funds. Malachi 3:10 is where God tells us that we can test Him in the practice of giving tithes. He promises that if we bring the entire tithe to the storehouse and don't hold back, He will not hold back either. Does that mean I had money overnight? Nope! What it did mean is that God matched my faithfulness. I always tithed before I paid anything else. Sometimes that meant that the power company had to wait for their money, or the water bill was late, but I trusted that God would cover me. My boundary was set that God came first. Every. Single. Time.

Eventually, I didn't have to choose between God and my bills. Through lots of hard work and diligence, I was able to pay my bills and tithe regularly. I was able to rest that there was enough money to feed the kids, tithe, and pay bills, and I was content with it.

I am merely sharing my experience in that trusting God and setting healthy boundaries has helped me come from disastrous situations and super hard times to a much more peaceful life. Please do not confuse my words with some prosperity-gospel-malarky or that God is a genie to serve us in any way. I tested God, through conviction, and found that He honored my sacrifice in deep, deep ways. Nothing was easy. There was no magical rescue. There was hard work, long days, diligence, getting up when I didn't want to, working when I didn't feel like it, giving up things I wanted for what I knew was right, juggling more time Tetris than I ever could imagine possible, plug and play to make every day happen, childcare and more childcare (especially after I became a widow!), one step in front of the other, little rest and little play, sacrifice upon sacrifice . . . and then one day . . . peace.

Here is the tricky part . . . I had to learn to focus on that peace! After toiling for so long, I'm talking a decade or more, it was hard to even notice the fruit that was happening. In spring 2020, my small Freedom group had a theme: Content with Goodness. We were going to learn to focus on being content with goodness. Sometimes in life we always want more, seek more, and have more, but when you are coming from little or less and you have to work so hard for more, more becomes the goal and the focus. I had to learn to pull back from that mentality and rest. Rest that the hard work had been completed. My first lesson was toiling and testing. My next lesson was to be content with goodness. If I had not shifted, then I might have missed the beauty of the second lesson. This is the stage I am in now, learning to be content with goodness. Was God still good if I was still where I was a decade or more ago? Yes. Part of the beauty of the journey with God is that He never seems to leave you where you started, no matter what journey lesson He has you on. So hold firm to your boundary to only enter into relationships that serve you. And hold firm to your relationship with God as you navigate your journey.

You won't walk my walk. It is unique to me and my Father. You will have your own walk to finding and implementing your boundaries. And as you find and hold your boundaries, you will grow and change in the ways God needs you to grow and change for His sake and to shine His light to all the world around you. Many may not understand, and that is OK. Hold your boundaries. Hold your lines. Seek God's face and His heart for you and love others well. When we have healthy boundaries, we are able to love so much more fully.

The journey may be long, and sometimes you may feel lost in it, but always keep your eyes focused on God, seeking His ways, and He will guide you. If you need help along the way, choose wisely who speaks into your life, but by all means, find someone who can help you along. We need each other and are meant to be in community. We are often stronger when we have a good support system. Sometimes we aren't born into those naturally, so you will have to create it for yourself, and that is quite beautiful because you can hand-select those that you know are safe and those who will treasure your heart.

I hope that you take the lessons from this book on family, culture, and faith practice boundaries, and dig into God and learn to set your boundaries so you can thrive like you have always dreamed of! Blessings to you! Let's pray one last time together.

Lord God,
This journey is new and exciting and a little, or a lot, scary. I am
learning to trust you, and I will begin to take the next step as you
show me how. I need your constant guidance, and I am trusting that
you will not leave me in this process. You have healthy boundaries,
and because you are active inside of me, I can do it too. Holy Spirit,
I need you to walk with me closely as I work out the kinks in my
relationships. I want to have healthy relationships and be able to love
people well. Please show me how to do this and reveal places in my
relationships that need boundaries that maybe I haven't seen before.
Thank you for your intimacy, Lord. Thank you for loving me enough
to die on the cross for my sins and to rise up out of the grave to be my
mediator and advocate. I am yours. Lead me. Guide me.
In Jesus' name,
Amen

Actionable Items:

- Now it's your turn. Practice your boundaries.
- Repeat the actionable items in this book every time you approach a new situation that makes your spirit, mind, and body uncomfortable.
- Pray scriptures daily. Write your favorite scriptures on notecards and place them where you will see them and say them every day.

Works Cited

Dictionary.com Unabridged Based on the Random House Unabridged Dictionary, © Random House, Inc. 2022

Bible.com NEW AMERICAN STANDARD BIBLE® NASB® Copyright © 1960, 1971, 1977,1995, 2020 by The Lockman Foundation A Corporation Not for Profit La Habra, CA All Rights Reserved www.lockman.org (NASB)

English Standard Version (ESV)   The Holy Bible, English Standard Version. ESV® Text Edition: 2016. Copyright © 2001 by Crossway Bibles, a publishing ministry of Good News Publishers.

New International Version (NIV)   Holy Bible, New International Version®, NIV® Copyright ©1973, 1978, 1984, 2011 by Biblica, Inc.® Used by permission. All rights reserved worldwide.

The Message (MSG) Copyright © 1993, 2002, 2018 by Eugene H. Peterson

About the Author

Stephanie Jordan is an author, teacher, cosmetologist, salon owner, passionate Jesus follower, and mother to five amazing kids. Her focus on boundaries and their benefits, interwoven within our freedom in Christ, ignited and unfolded in this book. Sharing her journey of God's faithfulness in the face of trials and teaching others the depth of God's love has become her life's work. She has been married, divorced and widowed. She is married to Kenneth Clay, and their family of nine kids combined resides in Birmingham, AL.

When she is not writing or speaking, you can find her riding a Harley Davidson Sportster 1200, flaunting new healthy gluten free recipes on her cooking blog/Facebook page (The Recovering Southerner), painting, reading, watching movies with the family, and spending time outdoors. You can find her on Instagram @therecoveringsoutherner and on Facebook https://www.faceb ook.com/authorstephaniejordan.

Other titles from Stephanie:

A Dose of Reality -Updated Release COMING SOON!

Please visit believinginboundaries.com for more information.

Please use #believinginboundaries so I can see your posts. :)

Can You Help?

Thank you for reading my book!

I really appreciate all of your feedback, and I love hearing what you
have to say.
I need your input to make the next version of this book
and my future books better.
Please leave me an honest review on Amazon or the store where
you purchased
the book, letting me know what you think of the book.
Image used from: https://thumbs.dreamstime.com/z/sleeping-c
at-vector-image-head-little-32368179.jpg

Thanks so much!

Made in the USA
Columbia, SC
06 July 2022